THE
UNDERGROUND GUIDE
TO
SAN FRANCISCO

The Underground Guide to San Francisco

Jennifer Joseph
EDITOR

MANIC D PRESS
SAN FRANCISCO

Dedicated to
the non-stop amazingness that keeps us here

EVER-LOVIN' DISCLAIMER: Just as almost everything in life is negotiable, so too everything is conditional and SUBJECT TO CHANGE without a moment's notice. A listing in this book does not imply endorsement. All opinions are those of the individual authors, and not necessarily those of the publisher or editor. All information is allegedly accurate as this goes to print but, hey, deal with it, okay? If you find something here that just ain't so, please be kind enough to let us know.

Thanks to the contributors, and to the Manic D production team: Lisa Taplin, Jennifer Goebel, and Heather Lewis. Thanks to Erick Gilbert, and to *Gearhead*, where Spike's Tenderloin Bar Crawl originally appeared.

drawings: Isabel Samaras   cover: Scott Idleman / BLINK

©1995 Manic D Press. All rights reserved. No part of this book may be reproduced in any manner whatsoever without written consent of the publisher, except for brief quotes used for review purposes. For more information, write to Manic D Press, Box 410804, San Francisco, CA 94141 USA

ISBN 0-916397-39-4

Library of Congress Cataloging-in-Publication Data

The underground guide to San Francisco / Jennifer Joseph, editor.
    p.   cm.
  Includes bibliographical references and index.
  1. San Francisco (Calif.)--Guidebooks.   I. Joseph, Jennifer.
F869.S33U53 1995
917.94'61--dc20   95-32489
                                              CIP

CONTENTS

FOREWARD!

San Francisco is the greatest city on the planet, right? Okay, now that we all agree, let's just say that this book is completely eclectic, outrageously opinionated, and was created with both visitor and resident in mind. I doubt that anyone who reads this will be like, "Yawn, same old tired tour book stuff..." I know there are things in here that few people know about, and besides it's a handy reference guide for living that ever-elusive affordable lifestyle here in America's most breath-taking city. It's the book I wish I had when I first moved here more than a decade ago.

Enjoy—

Jennifer Joseph

P.S. Do yourself a favor and buy a MUNI map, available at most corner stores. This map shows all bus lines, streetcars, cable cars, and more. Please note telephone area codes: 415 for SF, 510 for Berkeley and Oakland. Have fun!

COMING & GOING

CHEAP AIRLINE TICKETS • Check the bulletin board at **Rainbow Grocery** (1899 Mission) for random tickets and destinations. San Francisco's free weekly newspapers have advertisements for cheap travel agencies, as does the Sunday *Chronicle*'s Travel section. **Tower Air** (800-34-TOWER) has the cheapest one-way and roundtrip flights to and from New York. **Jupiter** (872-0845) and **UTL Travel** (583-5074) both offer low-cost courier flights to exotic destinations in Asia but limit travelers to two-week stays and one piece of carry-on baggage. **Southwest Airlines** (800-435-9792) usually offers a 2-for-1 deal anywhere they fly. **United** (800-241-6522) and **Alaska Airlines** (800-426-0333) also have 2-for-1 deals to Portland, Seattle, and/or Los Angeles out of Oakland. Regardless of airline, it's often cheaper to fly out of or into Oakland Airport, so check availability and prices.

GETTING TO & FROM THE AIRPORTS

SFO • Cheap and reliable if you don't have much baggage is the **SamTrans** bus #7F or 7B (800-660-4287). Runs often during the day, less frequently at night. Goes to and from the Transbay Terminal downtown at First & Mission Streets. Catch local **MUNI** (673-6864) buses to & from there. Shuttle vans are available to and from the airport, **Supershuttle** (558-8500) is a fairly reliable company. **Taxis** cost upwards of $25 dollars but up to five people can ride for one fare so it could be really cheap for a group of more than two.

OAKLAND • Take the **BART** (992-2278) train. A little more than an hour to SF. Inexpensive.

OTHER TRAVEL CONCEPTS

BUS • **Greyhound** (800-231-2222) comes and goes. So does the hound alternative, **Green Tortoise** (285-2441): call them for more info.

TRAIN • Ride the rails with **Amtrak** (800-872-7245).

DRIVEAWAY CARS • Someone else's vehicle, you pay for gas. Requires a refundable deposit. **AAA Transport** (342-9611).

COUCH SURFING ALTERNATIVES

Unless you have some pals in town, you're going to need someplace to crash. Even if you have pals in town, at some point they'll want their couch back.

JUST PASSING THRU • AYH (American Youth Hostels) operates 2 hostels in SF, a large one downtown (312 Mason; 788-5604) and a small one at Ft. Mason (771-7277). They're clean, safe, and cheap but have rules and offer little privacy. The **Green Tortoise Guest House** (490 Broadway; 834-1000) has single rooms for $20 and doubles for $34. They're usually booked up two weeks in advance so reservations are definitely recommended. Other hostels exist on Folsom Street between 7th & 8th Streets. For a righteous mini-vacation, ride a bicycle or the 76 MUNI bus (weekends only) out to the Marin Headlands youth hostel and spend the night. Fast and easy urban escape!

RESIDENTIAL HOTELS • Rent by the day, week, or month. Shared bathrooms usually. Run the gamut from decent to frightful. Other neighborhoods besides the Tenderloin featuring these low-cost accommodations include North Beach (**Sam Wong**-615 Broadway at Columbus; 781-6836, **Avenue Hotel**-524 Columbus at Stockton; 362-9861, **Europa**-310 Columbus at Broadway; 391-5779, **Golden Eagle**-402 Broadway; 781-6859) and South-of-Market. Poet/playwright Kathi Georges recommends the **Golden City Inn** (1554 Howard at 11th; 255-1110), located above her performance space, the Marilyn Monroe Memorial Theater. "Clean rooms and sheets," Kathi says, "And nobody's died there in years."

LONG TERM SHELTER • So you've decided to stay for awhile. For shared housing, check the ubiquitous bulletin board at Rainbow Grocery. The free weekly papers have listings, and there's always **Roommate Referral** (610A Cole at Haight; 626-0606). The best way to find your own apartment is to pick your desired neighborhood and look for 'For Rent' signs. Perseverance is key. Have cash ready for a deposit (usually first and last months, and a 'cleaning' deposit which usually equals one month's rent). Once you get your name on a lease, hang out for a while: rent control currently limits rent increases to less than 2% per year, and landlords must pay 5% interest annually on your security deposit. If you have questions about rent control or experience landlord problems, call the **SF Rent Board** (554-9550), **The Housing Committee** at Old St. Mary's (749-3700), or the **SF Tenants Union** (282-6622). If you move to a neighborhood that requires a parking permit to park your vehicle on the street for more than two hours, call 554-5000. Get one ASAP to avoid tickets or worse. Temporary permits are available if you're expecting visitors.

WHERE TO PUT PARENTS FOR UNDER $50 •

My parents usually don't appreciate my standard of living, though they're certainly grateful that I don't live with them anymore, and believe me, the feeling's extremely mutual. However, when they inevitably come to town, it's unlikely that they'll be making couch reservations, so here are a few non-motel alternatives. In the Sunset, close to the Haight is a terrific B&B called **Moffatt House** (431 Hugo; 661-6210), where rooms start around $35. The **Obrero Hotel** (1208 Stockton; 989-3960) in North Beach is barebones but clean for around $40. Similarly priced is the **San Remo Hotel** (2237 Mason; 776-8688) near Fisherman's Wharf.

THE HIPPEST HOTELS IN S.F. •

Here are a few joints that have distinguished themselves for whatever reasons. The **Phoenix Hotel** (601 Eddy; 776-1380) is where all the up-and-coming rock bands (like Sonic Youth, Soul Asylum, and everybody else on MTV) stay when they're in town. Rooms start at $89.00, and this is also the location of that ever-trendy restaurant, **Miss**

Pearl's Jam House, where you can eat dinner next to Soundgarden. Once a rock band (like Pink Floyd or Tom Petty, fer example) has made their first million, they stay at the **Clift** (Geary & Taylor; 775-4700) where special room rates start at $125. Have a cocktail in their fabulous **Redwood Room**, even if you can't afford to stay. Another swell joint is the **Triton Hotel** (342 Grant; 394-0500), which is decorated in post-PeeWee's Playhouse fashion, doubles start at $125.

EMPLOYMENT IDEAS

Get one outfit that consists of a dark skirt or trousers and a light-colored buttondown shirt. Walk into any temp agency listed under 'Employment' in the yellow pages and tell them you just moved here and were a (choose one or all): a. file clerk; b. receptionist; c. secretary; in your former hometown. Make up a list of where you worked and for how long before you go in (they won't call long distance to check). To be a receptionist, all you have to know is how to answer a phone. To be a file clerk, you have to know the alphabet. Once you're signed up with several temp agencies, call them relentlessly. Every day until they find you work. Don't get discouraged, it may take two weeks. Do take the first job they offer you, so they know you're serious about working. Even if it's picking

15

fleas off corporate chimps. Temp agencies pay weekly.

Apply the above general concept to restaurant work, except make up a history of being a: a. busperson; b. waitron; c. cook. Do not stop by during lunch or dinner hours. Tips=cash. No waiting for a paycheck.

If all else fails, you can always find employment in one of San Francisco's foremost time-honored occupations, the bike messenger. Think about it. You get to be outdoors all day, take breaks whenever you want. No bosses breathing down your neck. Even if you don't want to pedal, you could always be a dispatcher. Check the yellow pages under 'Delivery Service'.

For real, like, career kinda jobs, here are a few resources that may be worth checking out. **Experience Unlimited** (745 Franklin; 771-1776) a.k.a. Job Club is a service of the State of California Employment Development Department which helps people find jobs. **Alumnae Resources** (120 Montgomery; 274-4747) is a great source of job listings, classes, job counseling, workshops, etc. for women and men. **Media Alliance** (814 Mission; 546-6334) has a jobfile hotline for art, writing, publishing, video, film, etc. gigs. Media Alliance members are also eligible for group medical and dental insurance (what a concept!). There's a newsletter called *Opportunity NOCs* which lists job offerings at non-profit organizations. It's available at the **Foundation Center** (312 Sutter; 397-0902), a good place to do research if you're looking for free money for your project (whatever that project may be).

MAKING A FASHION STATEMENT

San Francisco has its own weather patterns — often the fog won't burn off til noon and will reappear with a vengeance around 3. Meteorological conditions can vary radically between neighborhoods — it may be 20° colder in the Haight than the Mission. Dressing in layers is suggested. For additional warmth or accessories, the following shops specialize in eclectic selections of wearables.

NEW • Everyone loves a bargain and bargains abound throughout this town. Outlet and discount shopping is different than cruising into Nordstroms where there are racks of everything in ten sizes and five colors. But with a little perseverance, amazing finds can be discovered. Favorite outlets include:

Esprit (499 Illinois) occasionally there are some incredible finds here, great kidswear. Shoes, handbags, etc.

The secret **Gap** outlet (2040 Chestnut) rules, but may be in flux. As of now, it's where the other Gap stores send the old stuff when new stuff comes in, and boy, is it marked down! And if the price goes down even further within the next two weeks, they'll give you a refund on the difference.

Burlington Coat Factory (899 Howard) has lots more than coats, tons of clothes for everyone — need a suit in a hurry? Go! **Shoe Pavilion** is in the same building.

There are many outlet stores south of Market in an area centered around Brannan & Bryant, and 2nd & 3rd Streets. Whether you're looking for a wedding dress (try **Jessica McClintock/Gunne Sax** outlet, 634 2nd St) or anything else, the area is certainly worth exploring.

Don't forget to check out **Marshalls** (901 Market) and **Ross** (799 Market), located one black apart, for some decent discounts off regular retail on clothes, shoes, and more. **Loehmann's** (222 Sutter) also has great discount prices, whether you need a formal evening gown or a casual jacket.

USED • You'll be stylin' in the finest duds if you eschew the department stores and frequent the following shops. Choose between funky and extra-funky.

Clothes Contact (473 Valencia) sells an ever-changing assortment of previously-owned clothing sold by the pound — sweaters, coats, shirts, etc.

Haight Street between Masonic and Stanyan has many recycled/vintage clothing stores — take a stroll, check 'em out — **Buffalo Exchange** (1555 Haight) will even buy choice clothes from you for cash or store credit.

Wacky thrift stores abound in the Mission — they're great for stocking a newly acquired living space with dishes, pots & pans, sheets, towels, etc. as well as clothes. Worth investigating are **Thrift Town** (2101 Mission) and **Community Thrift** (625 Valencia). **Salvation Army** (1509 Valencia) and **Goodwill** (2279 Mission) stores are not too far away.

FURNISHINGS • After a while having all of the furniture made out of milk crates and cinderblocks can get on your nerves. Besides the thrift stores, here are a few other good places to check out.

The basement of **Busvan** (900 Battery) has all kinds of tables, chairs, bookshelves, armoirs, etc. I found an incredible antique dresser there, complete with bevel-edged mirror for $50. Of course, I had to refinish it, but what's life without projects?

Next Express (1315 Howard) They got the new couches with the funky patterns for a lot less than you'd pay elsewhere. Spent my first Christmas bonus there getting real furniture.

Butterfield West (164 Utah at 15th; 861-7500) has an auction every three weeks with furniture, lamps, rugs, you-name-it. Plus it's just a cool place to check out, and put ridiculously low bids in on great stuff.

Economy Restaurant Fixtures (1200 7th St) has good kitchen chairs, plates, cups, pots and pans, etc.

Cottrell's (150 Valencia) has been around forever and they have tons of quality used furniture at good prices.

Second Hand Rose (18th St near Valencia) is a small shop with an eclectic mix of used furniture.

STUFF • This is the miscellaneous section, whether you're searching for hiking boots, a guitar, cheap film, or other stuff.

The **Depot** (1st and Mission) has tons of stuff — party supplies, kid stuff, kitchen stuff, odds and ends — for really cheap. I once got an awesome William Wegman poster, *Ray and Mrs. Lubner In Bed Watching TV*, for $1. If you don't know what I'm talking about, that's okay, too. Trust me on this one if you like getting stuff for cheap.

If you manage to find an apartment with hook-ups for a washing machine, you're in luck. Buy a used Maytag washer from a place like **Noel's Second Hand Appliances** (3178 17th St). Cost is around $125, and they'll deliver it for free or cheap. Do your laundry at 4 a.m. if you want, and you'll save mega-bucks over the local laudromat prices.

Located in Berkeley, **Subway Guitars** (1800 Cedar) has an awesome collection of used and vintage electric guitars. Amps, too. They also do repairs. In San Francisco, **Black Market Music** (1016 Howard) also has used equipment and does repairs.

For film, dark room supplies, and photo stuff, **Photographer's Supply** (576 Folsom) has the best prices in town.

If you enjoy the great outdoors, the **North Face Outlet** (1325 Howard) has a great selection of camping and hiking gear. For running, tennis, and basketball sneakers, **Big 5 Sporting Goods** (2159 Chestnut) has greatly reduced prices on name-brand footwear.

For sex toys and erotic goodies, go to **Good Vibrations** (1210 Valencia), which is geared toward women *and* men. Owned and operated by women, **Stormy Leather** (1158 Howard) specializes in bondage and fetish gear.

To purchase an affordable used computer that is guaranteed to work, visit the **Used Computer Store** (2440 Shattuck, Berkeley; 510-548-8686) or **Personal Computers For Less** (1309 Fillmore; 346-1692). For a reliable, affordable Internet/WWW connection call **Sirius Connections** (284-4700).

CHOWING DOWN

EATING OUT • There's an oft-repeated rumor that if everyone in San Francisco went out for dinner on the same night, there'd still be empty seats in restaurants. Truly, a person could eat out every night for years and never eat at the same place twice. The challenge is how to live it up for under $5. Beyond yer basic fast food dumps and franchised sandwich joints exists an intriguing cornucopia of international and American delicacies available to the uniquely sophisticated palates of local and visiting gourmets and gourmands.

BREAKFAST • For a mighty breakfast that'll keep you writing up a storm, many poets swear by the **New Dawn** (3174 16th St) Cafe. Serious potatoes! Blueberry pancakes at the **Pork Store Cafe** (1451 Haight) kick booty, and those folks are quite adept at keeping yer coffee filled. **Kate's Kitchen** (471 Haight) has got the happenin' scallion-cheese biscuits.

PIZZA • While there are many slices available all over town, **Golden Boy Pizza** (542 Green near Grant) in North Beach serves up the mondo slices at reasonable prices late into the night. **L'Osteria**'s (519 Columbus near Green) got unusual (try the porcini mushroom kind) slices at correct prices. **Escape from New York**'s (1737 Haight at Cole) got them tasty pesto slices, mighty palatable! **North Beach Pizza** (1499 & 1310 Grant) offers citywide 24-hour delivery, a great idea, but they serve whole pies only, no slices, but they'll provide free paper plates, hot peppers, and parmesan cheese if you request 'em.

FAMILY-STYLE ITALIAN • The coolest thing about family-style Italian restaurants is the quantity of food served. This kind of chow is not poodley, foo-foo California cuisine. No, at these joints they'll serve you bread, soup, salad, antipasto platter, and pasta, and then they'll ask you what you want for dinner. The answer is usually anything from chicken cacciatore to eggplant parmesan, etc. Try **Capp's Corner** (1600 Powell) or **The Gold Spike** (527 Columbus), where complete dinners start around $10.

SEAFOOD • The glorious $3 'Snapburger' from **Two Jacks Seafood** (401 Haight at Webster) is recommended by Michele C. "Real fish, real good," says Michele. Mike Kyle adds, "It's available to go only!"

FALAFEL, ETC. • The 'Mediterranean Plate' at **King of Falafel** (1801 Divisadero) is a deal — at $5, it feeds two. **Truly Mediterranean** (3109 16th St) has the great falafel pita sandwich.

MEXICAN • For the cheapest, most filling sustenance the substantial rice-and-bean burritos available at **El Buen Sabor** (699 Valencia) are king. At $1.80, they can't be beat. **Pancho Villa's** (3071 16th St at Valencia) super-vegetarian burrito is many burrito-lovers' preferred choice. They have a huge selection of combos. Try one made in a bright red tortilla, colored naturally by mild red chiles. For a less massive chowdown, their vegetarian tacos are piled high with the usual fixins plus guacamole & sour cream — $2.25! **Mission Villa** (2391 Mission at 20th St), which claims to be the oldest Mexican restaurant in San Francisco (founded in 1906), serves up a huge plate of food (rice, beans, salad, and choice of chile relleno, enchilada, etc.) + tortillas for $3.50. It also has groovy wooden booths, velvet paintings, and an excellent jukebox that features Hawaiian tunes among others. **Roosevelt's Tamale Parlor** (2817 24th St) serves up the righteous tamales.

NICARAGUAN • Kind of like Mexican, except different. **El Trebol** (3324 24th St) is a tiny restaurant where the most expensive thing on the menu (major grilled pork dinner, which includes salad, rice, beans, fried bananas, and salsa) costs $3.75. My favorite thing there are papusas, a variation of grilled cheese, served with a spicy Nicaraguan cabbage slaw. Awesome, and less than $1.

VIETNAMESE • Not for vegetarians, the $2 Vietnamese sandwich served at the **Vietnam Restaurant** (620 Broadway), a tiny shop a few steps away from City Lights bookstore features adventuresome meats with pickled vegetables rarely found on American varieties. Served on a sizable, warm French baguette, it's delicious. If you feel like you're coming down with a cold or the flu, have a bowl of Pho — it'll cure what ails you. **Tu Lan** (8 6th St) may look kind of seedy but the food rocks — check out the not fried spring rolls.

CHINESE • There are a zillion Chinese restaurants here. Huge amounts of food cheap. Look on the menu for noodles or 'Rice Plates' — that's where rice is served on the plate with your choice, instead of being brought to the table separately. Most places have Rice Plates listed at the back of the menu, usually for around $3. For major spicy food, try Hunan; for seafood, check out the Hong Kong style seafood places. During the day, stop in at a Chinatown deli, the one at Powell & Broadway is authentic and delicious. For satisfying, affordable Dim Sum to go, stop by a tiny storefront a few doors up Stockton at Broadway. The shrimp Har Gow kick butt! Another dim sum joint that also has very tasty ginger chicken over rice for $2 is **Broadway Dim Sum & Cafe** (684 Broadway near Stockton). It's open til 6:30 p.m. Chinatown also features late night chowdowns — **Yuet Lee** (1300 Stockton at Broadway) is open til 3 a.m. on weekends; **Silver Restaurant** (737 Washington) is open 24 hours.

KOREAN BBQ • For the best in interactive eating,

check out a Korean BBQ joint. Not cheap but total fun with pals, as the table is immediately covered in little dishes featuring bean sprouts, kim chee, tiny dried fish, and several less identifiable items. After deciding which kind of marinated meat you'd prefer (this type of restaurant is not recommended for vegetarians), a guy comes running out of the kitchen carrying a hibachi filled with blazing hot charcoal. He sets it on your table and the fun begins. Most of these places are on Geary Blvd in the Avenues, including **Kyoung Bok Palace** (6314 Geary).

INDONESIAN • The **Java** (417 Clement) restaurant in the Richmond has noodles with peanut sauce and satay really cheap — their spicy french fries are sheer delight.

BURMESE • **Burma Super Star** (309 Clement) has traditional tea leaves salad and an assortment of other unusually spiced goodies.

JAPANESE • When going to movies at the Kabuki, definitely eat at **Mifune** (in Japan Center, 1737 Post). Great soba and udon noodles, plus tempura, etc.

SUSHI • Craving the cold thrill of fabulous raw fish? Head over to **Nippon Sushi** (316 16th St), aka No Name Sushi because the sign doesn't have a name on it, a cozy favorite featuring the freshest ingredients and incredible prices.

VEGETARIAN • Veggies can have an awesome time eating out in this town: in Chinatown, there's **Lucky**

Creation (854 Washington). Then there's the **Shangri-La** (2026 Irving), out in the Richmond. **Amazing Grace** (216 Church) has great soups, salads, and sandwiches. **Real Good Karma** (501 Dolores) is a whole grain, mostly dairy-free kind of place. **Now and Zen** (1826 Buchanan) offers gourmet vegan fare, not cheap but not really pricey either. **The Ganges** (775 Frederick) features delicious all-vegetarian Indian cuisine.

BURGERS, ETC. • On the waterfront, nothing beats **Red's Java House** (Pier 30 & Embarcadero), double cheeseburger and a Bud for $1.95. The view is spectacular. **Mo's** (1322 Grant) in North Beach is the place to go when all the other restaurants have lines and you need to eat now. The vegetarian Grant Avenue sandwich, a combination of garlicky grilled mushrooms and fresh avocado served on foccacia, rules. Served with a heap of excellent fries for under $6.

ETHIOPIAN • Well, technically it's Eritrean food, but either way **Massawa** (1538 Haight) serves up the tasty giant plates of delicious, unusually-spiced chow. Served with a spongy flatbread called injera, this is totally fun dining. Use your fingers instead of a fork.

ET CETERA • Crepes galore and fresh-squeezed lemonade at **Ti Couz** (3108 16th St) — savory and sweet... Terrific. **Tom Peasant Pies** (4108 24th St) is amazing, serving one-person pies in both savory and sweet varieties for $2.25 each. Perfect for picnics. Ice cream sodas at the **St. Francis Fountain** (2801 24th

St) are the real thing, and harken back to days gone by. **Zante Pizza and Indian Cuisine** (3489 Mission) is the only restaurant in the universe where you can order a pepperoni pizza with a side order of raita. Mongolian barbecue is becoming all the rage, and **Kublai Khan's** (1160 Polk) is the only one in SF.

Free (Happy Hour) Food • Never underestimate how many cocktail franks it's possible to scarf down in the course of drinking one beer. Especially if the chow's free. **Cadillac Bar** (4-6:30 p.m., Monday-Friday, 325 Minna) has the giant buffet, drinks are under $3. **Eddie Rickenbacker's** (5-7 p.m., Monday-Friday, 133 Second St) has upscale chow, drinks are under $4. **Annie's Seafood Bar & Grill** (4:30-6:30 p.m., Monday-Friday, 20 Annie) has major snacks, drinks $4 and less. **MacArthur Park** (4-7 p.m., Monday-Friday, 607 Front) has got the buffalo wings, etc., drinks under $5.

All-You-Can-Eats • **Bottom of the Hill** (4-8 p.m., Sundays, 2742 17th St) has a killer AYCE Sunday afternoons barbecue for $3, with real live rock bands, too. **El Rio** (5-7 p.m., Fridays, 3158 Mission) has a Friday evening AYCE oyster bar. **Tonga Room** (5-7 p.m., Monday-Friday, Fairmont Hotel, 950 Mason) has a weekday happy hour $3 AYCE dim sum fest, complete with indoor rain shower. Tropical drinks are under $5. **Goat Hill Pizza** (300 Connecticut) has AYCE pizza and salad on Monday nights for $7.95. For meat-eaters, **Zim's** (1495 Market & Van Ness) has AYCE beef ribs on Mondays, and AYCE bbq chicken on Tuesdays. **Umeko** (Japantown) has a AYCE Asian seafood buffet every night for $15.95, including sushi, and **Giladon Sushi** (538 Valencia) offers AYCE sushi every night for $14.95. **Original Buffalo Wings** (663 Union) has AYCE guess what (buffalo wings, duh) for $5.99 on Wednesdays, 4–9 p.m.

OPEN 24 HOURS • At some point, you're gonna need to eat at 4 a.m. and you'll wonder what's open. In Chinatown, there's the **Silver Restaurant** (737 Washington), which has a sign out front announcing 24-hour Dim Sum. Trendy joints include the **Bagdad Cafe** (2295 Market), **Orphan Andy's** (3991 Market), and **Sparky's** (242 Church). Otherwise, the following places are open 'round the clock. None of 'em are great, but at 5 a.m. who cares? **Silver Crest Donut Shop** (340 Bayshore); **Lucky Penny** (2670 Geary); **Video Cafe** (21st Ave & Geary); **Pinecrest Restaurant** (401 Geary); **Denny's Japantown** (1700 Post); **International House of Pancakes** (2299 Lombard); **Zim's** (Market & Van Ness; 3490 California); **Mel's Diner** (2165 Lombard) is open 24 hours on Fridays and Saturdays. **North Beach Pizza** (433-2444) *delivers* 24 hours a day.

OPEN 24 HOURS/EAST BAY • Necessary info if you happen to be in Berkeley or Oakland. **JJ's Diner** (27th & Broadway) and the **Jack London Inn** (444 Embarcadero West) are both always open.

EATING IN • While man may be able to live on coffee and burritos alone, woman cannot. At some point, a home-cooked meal is gonna taste great, particularly if you're really broke.

Canned Foods Grocery Outlet (1717 Harrison) is often called the Museum of Lost Food, and it's my favorite place to shop in San Francisco.

Trader Joe's (9th & Brannan Sts) offers great products and prices for bread, milk, eggs, cheeses, and a whole lot more. Caution: may be habit-forming.

Castro Cheesery (427 Castro) has the best prices on coffee beans in the city. $3.50 for a pound of French Roast.

Civic Center Farmers Market (near Market between Leavenworth and Hyde) 9-5 on Wednesdays and 8-4 on Sundays. Local area farmers have whatever's in season for the cheapest prices around.

Embarcadero Farmers Market (on Embarcadero at the foot of Market St) 8 a.m.- 2 p.m. Saturdays in front of the Ferry Building. More upscale than the Civic Center, offers exotic varieties of potatoes, tomatoes, peppers and more.

Rainbow Grocery and General Store (1899 Mission) is one of the prime sources for organic produce. Also diverse bulk items. General store has Dr. Bronner's and other soaps and lotions in bulk, as well as vitamins, henna, candles, hemp wallets, and tons more.

FRESH PRODUCE • Among the cheapest places to buy vegetables in SF is Stockton Street in Chinatown. If you're willing to battle crowds of Chinese grandmothers, the prices are worth the effort.

24-HOUR GROCERY STORES • **FoodsCo** (14th St & Folsom); **Marina Safeway** (15 Marina Blvd); **Cala Foods** (Haight & Stanyan; 4201 18th St; California & Hyde; 6333 Geary Blvd). Remember, no beer or liquor is sold after 2 a.m.

WATERING HOLES

GOING UP • ACHIEVING MOMENTUM THROUGH PROPER CAFFEINATION • There are way too many awesome cafes where local poets have found inspiration at the bottom of a latte glass, so here are a few of the venerable coffeehouses with personality that transcend trendy twiddle-twaddle:

North Beach's oldest, crustiest **Caffe Trieste** (Grant Avenue & Vallejo) is visited almost daily by poet Jack Hirschman and many others. Get a cap to go and sit on the church steps across the street for unique neighborhood observations.

Sacred Grounds (2095 Hayes at Cole) in the Haight still has an authentic hippie vibe — serving up some cheap substantial food as well. Great for post–Park resuscitation. Open readings occur here every Wednesday evening, too.

The best people–watching is found at the **Horse Shoe** (566 Haight & Fillmore) in the lower Haight—practice your favorite expression of ennui among the young and the bored.

Mission poets have long frequented **La Boheme** (3318 24th St), an airy open room, with local art on the walls and good bulletin boards with notices of apartment shares, etc.

COMING DOWN • SHORTCUT TO INFAMY •

Some of the City's most famous denizens have built a career upon excessive alcohol intake—where would Kerouac be without years perched on barstools? Banish the thought. Following is a sample of some non-foo-foo drinking establishments (hint: most are better on weeknights).

North Beach's best-known litbars are within stumbling distance of City Lights: **Spec's** (12 Adler) is full of cranky poets on any given night—the place is crammed full of weird old memorabilia, including some of the customers. Be a poet or just look like one parked under a large portrait of James Joyce on the balcony upstairs at **Vesuvio** (255 Columbus). Key seating is upstairs by the front window at sunset when the Broadway lights come on—pints of Anchor Steam are an essential part of the total experience!

When in the Mission, fall off your barstool at the **Uptown** (200 Capp) or the **Dovre Club** (3541 18th St). Poet David West recommends visiting the **Wild Side West** (424 Cortland) on a weeknight—he says be sure to check out the toilet collection in the backyard. West also endorses Monday nights at **El Rio** (3158 Mission)—drinks cost $1!

On a sunny day, enjoy an industrial harbor view of the shipyards from the deck of the **Mission Rock Resort** (817 China Basin).

San Francisco is home to several micro-breweries, where beer is brewed on the premises and changes seasonally. Check out **Twenty Tank Brewery** (316 11th St) in the heart of nightclub-land, or the **San Francisco Brewing Company** (155 Columbus) in North Beach, with its turn-of-the century interior. Babyface Nelson was nailed here by the Feds long before it was a microbrewery.

If you really feel like doing something different, drinking at the **Motherlode** (1002 Post) is like being in a John Waters movie. Also recommended is the **Club Charleston** (10 6th St) for cheap cocktails in a classic dive bar. For extensive dive descriptions, check out Spike's *Tenderloin Bar Crawl*, beginning on page 95.

FREE & CHEAP ENTERTAINMENT

OUTDOOR FUN & SPORTS • The fact that the weather tends to be eternally Spring-like lends itself to activities in the Great Outdoors. While destinations like Yosemite, Big Sur, Point Reyes, and Mt. Tamalpais are within spitting distance, here are a few that are a tad closer to home.

For a great day trip of outdoor adventure, take the **Ferry to Angel Island** (546-2896) for a picnic and hike. Weekends only. Or just hop a ferry to Sausalito or Oakland any day of the week.

During summer weekends through October, the **SF Shakespeare Festival** (666-2221) presents free Shakespeare plays in Golden Gate Park.

During the summer months, the **Stern Grove Festival** (252-6252) presents free programs at Golden Gate Park's Stern Grove by notables like the Preservation Hall Jazz Band; the SF Ballet, the SF Opera, and more. Bring a blanket and a picnic.

During baseball season, sit in the bleachers for a **Giants game** at Candlestick (excuse me, 3Com) Park. Buy tickets when you get there. Take the MUNI Ballpark Express (call 673-MUNI for info) and enjoy an afternoon in the sun and fog. Enjoy a ballpark tofu dog with extra mustard and sauerkraut!

Grab your clubs and play a few holes at a San Francisco public **Golf** Course. Call 666-7070 for info.

Tennis, anyone? SF also has public tennis courts. Call 751-7300 for info.

FREE WALKING TOURS • Dozens of free walking tours are conducted every month by **City Guides**, a volunteer service of Friends of the San Francisco Public Library. Most walks take about an hour and a half. Tours are available for almost every neighborhood in the City, including Chinatown, North Beach, Pacific Heights mansions, and a whole bunch more. Call 557-4266 for detailed information, including time schedules and starting points.

The **Zoo** is free the first Wednesday of every month—visit the animals with some kids for a real thrill.

• The following **MUSEUMS** are FREE the first Wednesday of every month:

EXPLORATORIUM. A hands-on science museum that's uniquely amazing. (Lyon & Marina; 561-0360)

CARTOON ART MUSEUM. Everything from Krazy Kat to R. Crumb as long as it's cartoons, comics or comix. (814 Mission; CAR-TOON)

STEINHART AQUARIUM. Home of the godlike Fish Roundabout and more. Not to be missed. (Golden Gate Park; 750-7145)

DeYOUNG MUSEUM. Art. Changing exhibits. Also free the first Saturday of every month from 10 til noon. (Golden Gate Park; 750-3600)

MUSEUM of MODERN ART is free the first TUESDAY of every month, and offers reduced admission on Thursday evenings after 5, and they're open til 9. (Third and Howard)

MORE ART • Art Gallery Openings are a good source of FREE food, drink, and sometimes even interesting art. Traditionally, the first Thursday of every month is when many receptions happen. 49 Geary Street is home to four separate galleries, and 250 Sutter has three. Check listings in the *Bay Guardian*, or the Sunday *Chronicle*'s Pink Section for more.

More Fun • Everybody has different ideas about what's fun, but here are some tried and true suggestions.

Rock'n'Bowl is great bowling entertainment for a foggy afternoon—cheap drinks are served there, too. (1855 Haight at Stanyan; 826-2695)

Visit the **Basic Brown Bear Factory** (444 DeHaro & Mariposa; 626-0781) and see teddy bears being made.

Check out **Golden Gate Fortune Cookie Company** (56 Ross Alley between Jackson & Washington; 781-3956) and see fortune cookies being made (how *do* they get those little pieces of paper in there?)

Take a tour of the **Anchor Steam Brewing Company** (1705 Mariposa; 863-8350), available by appointment only. Book 3-4 weeks in advance. The tasting room awaits at the end of the tour.

Swim a few laps at one of San Francisco's public **Swimming** Pools (North Beach: Lombard & Mason, 274-0200; Mission: 19th & Linda, 695-5002; Richmond/Haight: Arguello Blvd, 666-7014). Call for hours.

The **Public Library** is exceptional—visit the Special Collections department for rare poetry and more. (Larkin & MacAllister; 557-4400)

The **San Francisco Ballet** (Opera House at 401 Van Ness), when in season, sells balcony seats for $7.50 each

—whatta deal for symphonic music, great dance, terrific costumes, and excellent buns!

Ride the **cable cars** late at night when they're almost empty (they run til midnight). Total fun riding on the outside singing show tunes in the wind. Tell the conductor you can't find your Fastpass—he might let you ride for free. Then again, he might kick you off immediately if you don't have your money ready. Oops!

COOL MUSIC AT CHURCH • **Church of John Coltrane** features jazz with prayers (351 Divisadero; 621-4054). **Glide Memorial** (330 Ellis) has an uplifting gospel choir. **Ancient Tridentine Catholic Church** (130 11th Ave; 585-2402) swings to Gregorian chants.

ALMOST FREE BUS TOURS • Certain MUNI routes cut all the way across San Francisco and if you secure a window seat, you can experience a mighty fine San Francisco tour for $1, roundtrip with transfer. Recommended is the **22 Fillmore** line which rolls from the Marina waterfront through Pacific Heights, the Mission, Potrero Hill and beyond, all the way to Third Street. The **29 Sunset** goes out to Baker Beach and offers some great views, as does the **39 Corbett**. Buy a MUNI map at most corner grocery stores.

GET SMART • Just so you know, San Francisco **City College** offers continuing education classes for cheap, and they're certainly extra-swell! Everything from pottery to botany is taught at campuses spread throughout the City, so if you feel like your brain is beginning to rot (or if you just want something to talk about at cocktail parties), call 239-3000 for a course catalog.

WHAT TO DO AT 5 A.M. • When you've done too much cheap speed and feel the urge to keep moving, head over to **Japantown Bowl** (Post & Webster). They're setting up the pins 24 hours a day.

GOING OUT

SPOKEN WORD • Poetry readings constitute one of the best entertainment values in the City because they're free. Maybe you'll even get to participate in a poets' brawl. You might even get to hear some great writing and/or profoundly lame haikus. Each reading has its own distinct flavor and characteristics. All have featured readers in addition to open mikes, get there early if you'd like to participate. For even more readings, check out the Spoken Word listings in the free weeklies or pick up *Poetry Flash*, a free monthly poetry info source distributed at independent literary bookstores.

SUNDAY: **Paradise Lounge**. Upstairs. 8 p.m. 21 & over. 1501 Folsom; 861-6906.
MONDAY: **Chameleon**. 9 p.m. 21 & over. 853 Valencia.

WEDNESDAY: **Jammin' Java**. 8:00 p.m. All ages. At Waller & Cole Sts.

FRIDAY: **Cafe International**. 8 p.m. All ages. 508 Haight at Fillmore; 552-7390.

MUSIC • Lots of clubs have music for little or no door charge, call ahead to find out how much and who's playing. Also, *always* bring your I.D. to prove you're over 21 (even if you're 30). This is by no means a complete list of venues, just the ones we think are worth mentioning.

BLUES

The **Blue Lamp** is a funky little dive featuring blues and more. (561 Geary; 885-1464).

Jack's is a mellow bar with blues on the weekends. (1601 Fillmore; 567-3227)

ROCK

Bottom of the Hill hosts local and indie touring rock bands. (1233 17th at Missouri; 626-4455)

The **Chameleon** has local punk bands and good beer on tap. (853 Valencia; 821-1891).

Covered Wagon aka CW Saloon has live rock bands on some nights, and DJs on the others. Low-key and loud and it has nothing to do with country music. (917 Folsom; 974-1585)

DNA is a fun place to go dancing, and is open after-hours, though no alcohol after 2 a.m. (375 11th St, 626-1409)

The **Fillmore** is one of the most renown concert

venues in the U.S. and is still an amazing place to see bands. Nationally-known bands usually. (1805 Geary; 346-6000)

Great American Music Hall, with its majorly stylin' interior, is one of the all-time great places to see live music. (859 O'Farrell; 885-0750)

Hotel Utah is a low-key bar with original music by local bands (Bryant & 4th St; 421-8308)

Kilowatt is the most recent incarnation of the rock club on 16th Street. Local and indie touring bands. (3160 16th St; 861-2595)

The **Paradise Lounge** is a bar and nightclub divided into several rooms featuring pool tables, a cozy fireplace, and three stages. Local bands and more. (1501 Folsom; 861-6906)

The **Purple Onion** has surf, punk, and garage bands of all colors and flavors. Plus it's got a great history. (140 Columbus; 398-8415)

Slim's is a rather nondescript room where some really great bands play. Bands playing here today will often be playing a bigger venue next time around. Mostly national, some local. (333 11th St, 621-3330)

Jazz

Elbo Room (647 Valencia) has lots of cool jazz upstairs and a decent bar downstairs.

Up & Down Club (1151 Folsom) has more jazz, plus it's partially owned by supermodel Christy Turlington.

Cavernous DJ Dance Clubs

Ten15 changes every night of the week, house, funk, '70s, whatever. (1015 Folsom; 431-1200)

Trocadero Transfer has goth, industrial, etc. etc. Wednesday nights is Bondage-A-Go-Go, wear your favorite peek-a-boo leathers. Occasional live shows. (520 4th St; 995-4600)

Sound Factory attracts many suburbanites but if you gotta dance... (525 Harrison; 543-1300)

Townsend keeps the beat going past 2 a.m. and into the wee hours. (177 Townsend; 974-1156)

RAVES

Most of the rave scene has moved to the clubs just mentioned, but for time and place details, pick up a handful of colorful invites at **Housewares** (1322 Haight).

MOVIES • There are dozens of movies showing at any given moment in this town. Here are a few venues for checking out the silver screen.

The **Roxie** (16th St & Valencia; 863-1087) and **Red Vic** (1659 Haight; 668-3994) have new independent films as well as repertory showings. As does **The Castro** (429 Castro; 621-6120), one of San Francisco's grandest movie theaters, which even has a guy playing the Mighty Wurlitzer. The orchestra pit in the front of the theater swallows the Wurlitzer and guy.

The **Kabuki** (Post & Fillmore; 931-9800) movie theaters have half-price matinees all afternoon — 8 different screens, such a choice.

San Francisco **Cinematheque** (558-8129) is in its 34th season of presenting experimental and non-commercial films at majorly affordable prices. Screenings are usually Sunday evenings at the SF Art Institute (800 Chestnut) or Thursday evenings at the Yerba Buena Center for the Arts (701 Mission at Third).

The **Geneva Drive-In** (next to the Cow Palace; 587-2884) has several screens and is San Francisco's only drive-in. Take a six-pack and climb in the back seat.

On the other end of the spectrum, SF is home to two micro-cinemas, the **Casting Couch** (950 Battery; 986-7001) and **Total Mobile Home Micro Cinema** (51 McCoppin; 431-4007). Call ahead to see if there's space on the sofa for one more person.

ATA also known as Artists Television Access (992 Valencia; 824-3890) screens underground videos and films, as well as offering workshops and renting video editing equipment to aspiring filmmakers.

THEATER, DANCE & PERFORMANCE • STBS, aka San Francisco Ticket Box Office Service (Union Square, on Stockton bet. Post & Geary) has half-price tickets for that evening's mainstream and alternative theater performances. Stop by and see what's available.

Ft. Mason is home to both the **Magic Theater** (441-

8822) and the **Cowell Theater** (441-3400), call for programming details.

Theater Artaud (450 Florida; 621-7797) always has something going on, be it dance, performance, or an experimental circus.

Climate Theater (252 9th St; 626-9196) hosts the annual Solo Mio Festival and other productions. Workshops are also offered.

LunaSea (2940 16th St #216C; 863-2989) features women-only cabaret, performance art, readings, and more.

The Marsh (1062 Valencia; 826-5750) hosts solo performers performing works in progress and finished works as well on Monday nights and weekends.

Intersection for the Arts (446 Valencia; 626-2787) is a community-oriented space, complete with art gallery and theater. Programs include drama, dance, poetry slams, and more traditional readings and writing workshops.

Josie's Juice Joint and Cabaret (3583 16th St; 861-7933) offers an astounding variety of queer cabaret, comedy, drama, spoken word, you-name-it. A fabulous establishment.

WHERE TO HAVE A POETIC EXPERIENCE

While inspiration lurks everywhere and anywhere in this town, here are a few places that have a built-in appreciation factor — great for contemplation and composition. May your muse always broadcast loud and clear.

Ocean Beach (at the end of Golden Gate Park) is huge and accessible for long windswept walks, peering into the vastness of ocean and air — always a relief after an overdose of humanity.

Near Ocean Beach are the ruins of **Sutro Baths** — all that remains of a once thriving civic wonder from the turn of the last century — San Francisco's own reminder of past glory and fallen civilization. Wander among the ruins and ponder. (Near Cliff House & end of Geary)

Beyond the throngs and hordes of Fisherman's Wharf is **a quiet pier** located behind Scoma's restaurant (Pier 47, Fisherman's Wharf) — perfect for that 'Sittin on the Dock of the Bay' kind of mood, a place to watch sailboats, harbor seals, Alcatraz, the Golden Gate bridge, and all of that corny stuff.

Nearby at the end of the Fisherman's Wharf area is **Aquatic Park** (Beach & Hyde), where on weekends drummers drum and humans lie around like seals basking in the sunshine.

For quiet contemplation near the Haight, the **Strybing Arboretum** (Lincoln & 9th) is a botanical garden in Golden Gate Park that can provide many hours of thoughtful solace. The humid **Conservatory** (Arguello & Fulton) is filled with strange tropical plants. There's even a small herd of **buffalo** who are always looking for company. Golden Gate Park is full of amazing discoveries.

Jack Early Park (Grant between Chestnut & Francisco) is a tiny promontory with a sweeping view of the Bay, perfect for solitude or a secret rendezvous.

Climb any hill — Telegraph, Russian, Nob, Potrero, Twin Peaks, Bernal Heights, 17th Street, wherever — and look at the view when you catch your breath.

OTHER HELPFUL INFO

The local alternative weeklies, the **SF Weekly** and the **SF Bay Guardian**, are free and come out every Wednesday. Check 'em out for updated entertainment listings, and handy-dandy discount coupons for restaurants!

The **Main Post Office** (go out on 3rd past Army, and take a left on Evans, go half a block til you see the sign) is awesome. On weekdays, the counter's open til 8:30 p.m. and mail gets picked up until 11 p.m. weekdays and Saturdays, essential if you desperately need something postmarked by a certain date. If you're searching for a **zip code**, call 284-0755.

If you want to adopt a pet, check with your landlord first, and then go to the **City Animal Shelter** (1200 15th at Harrison). They have a huge assortment of cats and dogs as well as guinea pigs, birds, and hamsters. The adoption fees are very reasonable, and these animals will be put to sleep if no one takes them home. The **SPCA** (2500 16th St) is right around the corner, if you don't see one you like at the City Shelter.

Consumer Action (777-9635) helps people who've been screwed over. They can refer you to the appropriate complaint and licensing bureaus.

Consumer Credit Counseling Service (788-0288) helps people who have maxed out their credit cards and are up to their eyeballs in debt.

EMERGENCY INFORMATION

Dial 911 from any telephone for **police**, **fire department**, or an **ambulance**.

24-Hour **Suicide Prevention** Hotline: 781-0500

24-Hour **Domestic Violence** Hotline: 800-540-5433

24-Hour **Rape Treatment** Center: 821-3222.
SF Women Against Rape (24 Hours) 647-7273.

24-Hour **Pharmacy**: Walgreen's (498 Castro; 861-6276. 3201 Divisadero; 931-6415)

24-Hour **Gas Stations**: Downtown-Shell (5th St & Folsom); Union 76 (1st St & Harrison). Haight-Chevron (Fell & Masonic). Richmond-BP (19th Ave & Judah); Shell (Geary & 9th Ave). Sunset-Chevron (19th Ave & Irving).

If your car's been towed, dial 553-1235. The evil address of shitty, most-hated City Tow is 1475 Mission, but you have to get a release from a police station before those lousy bastards'll release your unfortunate auto, after making you pay a king's ransom.

If your pet becomes deathly ill, or is hit by a car, take it to **Pets Unlimited Veterinary Hospital** (2343 Fillmore; 563-6700). They offer 24-hour emergency services, as well as a low-cost walk-in vaccination clinic for dogs and cats every Thursday.

HEALTH & WELLBEING

Women's Needs Center — 1825 Haight St 487-5607 - Providing medical support services for women's health concerns, including pregnancy testing, birth control, HIV testing, STD treatments, etc. in a personal atmosphere. Sliding scale.

HIV/AIDS — For up-to-date, accurate information about prevention, testing, and early care and treatment of HIV/AIDS, call the AIDS Hotline, 863-2437. To obtain information about getting tested anonymously, or to make an appointment, call the AIDS Health Project's appointment line, 554-9888. The San Francisco AIDS Foundation provides free direct and specialized services to persons living with AIDS and symptomatic HIV in San Francisco, 864-5855.

Haight-Ashbury Free Medical Clinic — (1698 Haight; 487-5634) provides low-to-no cost basic medical services and detox programs. Call ahead, appointments are extremely recommended.

Alcoholics Anonymous — 621-1326

SF Mental Health Association — (921-4044) provides referrals and emergency information.

General Hospital — (1001 Potrero; 206-8000) can be a nightmare from hell, but if you don't have insurance, go there in an emergency.

University of the Pacific Dental School (2155 Webster; 929-6501) — Free and low-cost services if your teeth are messed up, or even if they just haven't been cleaned in awhile.

SF Department of Social Services — (557-5000) Food stamps, general assistance (also known as GA, or welfare).

Northern California Community Services Council — (772-4357) provides information on free food, shelter, and other services in case everything falls apart at once.

In the miserable case where you need a lawyer, try the **SF Neighborhood Legal Assistance Foundation** (627-0220) or the Bar Association of SF's Referral & **Volunteer Legal Services Program** (764-1616).

WHERE'S THE PARTY?

BY BRAD WIENERS

San Francisco loves to celebrate. The following events are free, fun, and a helluva way to meet people. Or just go out and be part of the thronging masses..... There are many more happenings than just the ones here, so keep your eyes peeled.

BAY TO BREAKERS (Third Sunday in May)

Talk about mobilizing a populace: on the third Sunday of May, the San Francisco *Examiner* and a host of other sponsors have arranged for 100,000 athletes, weekend warriors, jog-walkers, joggers for-a-day, and just plain freaks to run from Howard and Spear Streets, one block from the San Francisco Bay, all the way out to Ocean Beach. The course is about 7.6 miles, a perfect length since most can make it without much training. (At least, that's the only way I have ever done it).

Bay to Breakers is also famous for its costumes, both individual and team, nudity (there's always a few running free and bouncy), and the occasional beer jock, who runs alongside his keg in a shopping cart. Bands every few blocks provide inspiration. Less fitness-minded folks gather along the course to cheer and jeer and party. Along with the jogging, the event is something of a seven mile brunch. About the only part of the event that can be a drag is at the start, where everyone bottlenecks into one intersection and will often stand stock still for five to ten minutes before inching towards the start line. Still, as long as it's not too cold, the start line has its amusements: runners with shark fins on their heads move through the crowd creating a polychromatic *Jaws* effect; someone invariably breaks out the tortillas and the air becomes filled with corn and flour Frisbees. Of course, if you're even slightly competitive you run the whole way even though you haven't so much as run for a bus in weeks, just to be sure to finish ahead of your out-of-town guests.

CARNAVAL (Last Weekend in May)

Clearly, San Francisco can't claim to have originated Carnaval, the fiesta that turns Rio De Janeiro inside out each year in March, and inspires a certain amount of creative and sexual promiscuity the rest of the year. San Francisco's Carnaval transforms many of the more reckless city blocks into an epicenter of mirth and whimsy. The costumes are incredible and the samba music is contagious. Dozens of festive floats blaring Latin music and ferrying scantily clad men and women set the stage for hours of entertainment including bandstands, thrill rides, every kind of food imaginable from canvas-walled booths, clothes, beers, margaritas, dancing in the streets, and sunburns that last for two weeks.

GAY, LESBIAN, BISEXUAL & TRANSGENDER FREEDOM DAY PARADE (Third Weekend in June)

Every year the newspapers publish a number, 350,000, for example, meant to represent the number of folks who turn out for San Francisco's Gay Pride Day, and ever year we locals wag our heads knowing what an impossible project it is for anyone to guesstimate the crowds that gather to cheer, cry, goggle, and come out.

In San Francisco, one need not be gay to attend. The parade is most definitely for the entire family, Dykes on Bikes and all. In 1995, Newt Gingrich's half-sister made quite a splash, taking a turn as Grand Marshal of the parade, but the parade, for all its entertainment value, is mostly about an impossible-to-count number of private lives declaring their freedom from narrow-mindedness. There are tears, of course, and more than a few middle fingers flying high (usually directed at the local ineffectual politicians), but mostly flags, banners, and insignia that affirm life, love and freedom. Needless to say, much of the real fun takes place the nights before and after the main event ...

HAIGHT STREET FAIR (Early Summer)
FOLSOM STREET FAIR (Late September)

Two sartorial clues will help you forever distinguish these two street fairs, (and if you ever go, you'll never have any problem distinguishing them). Haight=Tiedye. Folsom=Leather.

If one is psychedelic, and the other tight and bulging, what unites them is fantasy. Unlike most street fairs which are merely funkier versions of the shopping arcades that line the street everyday, at the Haight and Folsom street fairs folks come out to do what they always wanted to do in public but were afraid to show.

Where else, for example, could you see all those piercings and butt cracks smiling at you as you can on Folsom? Look, you'll exclaim, there goes porn star Jamie Gillis! Up on Haight, the acid-laced punch and music pours all day. As with Bay to Breakers, a lot of folks visit from out of town for the Haight Street fete and the result is a theme park version of the Summer of Love, set to a contemporary vibe.

SF MIME TROUPE IN THE PARK (begins on July 4)

For more than 30 years, the San Francisco Mime Troupe (which doesn't do mime) has performed original musical theater pieces throughout San Francisco's parks free of charge. Summer in Dolores Park (in the San Francisco's oldest district, the Mission), is an ideal setting for the Mime Troupe's satiric shows. Often political in content, the shows are, in that cliched phrase, "fun for the whole family," but also fun for those attending with a surrogate family of roommates or with no family at all. My recommendation: make the

Mime Troupe part of an entire day outdoors. Bring a cooler. Soccer Ball. Blanket. Some poems. Between the wit of the Mime Troupe, the sun, the grass, the dogs, and the views back at the city (I'm thinking Dolores Park here), you can restore at least a little of your sanity.

HALLOWEEN IN THE CASTRO (October 31)

Like a street fair only it doesn't even begin until after dark! Halloween in the Castro is for anyone with a touch of Peter Pan syndrome or, better still, for those who consider spooky, scary, and sexy trick-or-treating a serious, adult activity. You don't have to be queer, you just have to like to dress up. I once wrote my friend a letter with this account:

"Somewhere nearby a rain dance or maybe it's just repercussions from Halloween in the Castro. That was last night. They close off the Castro and it becomes a swarming, pagan morass of polysexuality and demonic grins. If there is one event that will make one write like Ginsberg, out of breath, double helix retro avalanche of adjectives, it's the Castro on Halloween. A carnival. Costumes. Hormones. Dancing in the Streets. Bodies pressed close like in the pit at a concert."

ST. STUPID'S DAY PARADE (April Fools Day)

On April 1st for each of the last seventeen years, Bishop Joey of the First Church of the Last Laugh has led the St. Stupid's Day Parade, a zany, parodic assembly that snakes through San Francisco's financial district celebrating St. Stupid and mocking the institutions of commerce. Most years, the parade concludes on the steps of the Pacific Stock Exchange, where sermons are given and everyone removes a sock for the "Pacific Sock Exchange." It should come as little surprise to learn that many go home with just one sock, as the sock exchange often digresses into a sock-ball fight. Recently, April Fools fell on a Saturday, so Bishop Joey led his minions up Columbus Avenue (from the Transamerica Pyramid) to Washington Square Park.

On hand with their massive Doggie Diner head was The San Francisco Cacophony Society, a rather well-organized group of free spirits and anarchists. They all wear chef's hats with droopy dog ears and call themselves the Dog-minican Order. Vanessa, a friend of mine, was on top of the Doggie head and threw bewildered passersby MilkBone dog biscuits. I caught one. They don't taste half-bad.

Author and Merry Prankster Ken Kesey served as Grand Marshal. Another acclaimed author, Howard Rheingold, wore polka-dotted pajamas and a rubber anteater nose, and pushed the non-running El Dorado carrying Kesey. (This is St. Stupid's Day, after all). At Columbus and Broadway, someone suddenly ordered the parade to take a nap in the road. We did.

By the time the Parade reached Washington Square Park, the crowd was as hungry as a Sunday school class anticipating the promised snack-religious services, but first Bishop Joey swore everyone in to the First Church of the Last Laugh. We raised the wrong hand and repeated after him, and then were informed of many of St. Stupid's profundities, including, "The nearer you get, the closer you are."

CRITICAL MASS (last Friday of every month)

Bike messengers, mountain bikers, bicycle commuters, and riders of every variety unite to stop the traffic on the last Friday of every month in a rally promoting the use of bikes instead of cars. It's a fun, politically charged, though leisurely, ride through the most congested areas of San Francisco. Meeting at the foot of Market Street (bring your own bike), hundreds of anti-automotive two-wheelers peacefully ride together down Market Street. The riders hand out flyers about the harm of cars and the benefits of bicycling. The ride lasts about an hour and people generally split off for rides across the Golden Gate Bridge or to the Beach. It's a great way to meet fellow bikers and block traffic for an hour. It pisses off the cops and the commuters, but that's half the fun, right?

BURNING MAN (Labor Day Weekend in Nevada)

If the Labor Day event known formally as the Black Rock Festival and informally as "Burning Man" had a bumper sticker, it might read, "A Working Class Freak Is Something to Be." Now in its 11th year, hundreds of San Franciscans, including those who stage the event, convoy out the Black Rock Desert in Nevada for a weekend of bizarre fun. For some, it has become the biggest ritual event of the year, Christmas in September.

Begun as a way to exorcise himself from a romantic break-up, Larry Harvey first erected and burned a wooden man on San Francisco's Baker Beach in 1985. When the man's immolation began attracting crowds, authorities frowned on the fledgling ritual and Harvey was forced to find a new location. He allied himself with the San Francisco Cacophony Society and together they moved the show to Nevada. The event quickly became a gathering of the tribes, each group adding their own events and installations to round out a full weekend of bizarre attractions. Nothing less than a sudden community of a few thousand gathered to witness the annual torching of a forty-foot man constructed of wood and neon.

Despite all the creative lunacy, nothing surpasses the experience of a soak and mud bath at the desert hot springs, thirty minutes to the north. Whether at dawn or during the heat of the day, the thermal warmth and sulfuric steam clears the head and soothes the body. Folks smear the black and gray mud on each other, play like children, and admire each other's physiques like adults.

Last year, the weekend's climax lived up to its billing: the burning man sent the onlookers into a frenzied circle dance, everyone twirling, hugging, tripping, laughing, and throwing sacrificial clothes and totems into the blaze. Then, with everyone's energy at a peak, Shark Bait, a percussion-driven band that had erected a stage just to the side of the pyre, distributed car fenders, corrugated tin and aluminum, engine blocks, and other scrap metal and showered the crowd with three boxes worth of drumsticks. Soon, with the flames still beating at our backs, several hundred beat out a new, other-worldly rhythm. The morning after, with tents collapsing and the crowd draining away, one begins to distrust one's memories: the costumed six-foot rabbit that asked you if you'd seen his ears, the purple-pink light of flares illuminating the desert floor, the primal screams, murmurs and spiders of sparks. As you pull away and the camp recedes and then vanishes in a cloud of dust, it's easy to think it was all a tremendous hallucination. For more information, write to: Burning Man, P.O. Box 420572, San Francisco, CA 94142-0572; or call 985-7471.

READING FRENZY

BY JON LONGHI

If all the ink in the world were to suddenly vanish, publishers in San Francisco would print things in their own blood. This same kind of barnacle tough determination extends to the fog city's underground bookstores. Relentlessly alternative, dismissing the New York Times Best Seller List and Publisher's Weekly top ten as mere hallucinations of a brain dead society, most local book and magazine shops instead surf the fringes, always looking for new mind candy to please the diverse plethora of subcultures which make up the social body of this city. From highbrow academic theory to the lowest, most filthy pornography, they offer it all. Most retailers are also supportive of the local publishing community to a degree that few other stores around the country are. Many even go so far as to stock handmade editions and zines. For out-of-towner and resident alike, there is the special treat of obtaining raw literary and artistic gems they can find no place else.

The feverish pitch of creative activity in the Bay Area often leads one to believe it is some kind of hallucinogenic art colony. On a percentage basis, San Francisco and its environs probably crank out more art than any other city on the planet. This imagination extends to the merchandisers themselves. Stores in this town are downright gaudy with personality. Many places are quasi-entities combining things like bone collections, tattooists, hair salons, books, tapes, fortune telling, and periodicals, all in one establishment. Oh yes, coffee is also usually involved. For a lover of books, many a listless afternoon can be euphorically killed poking through the arcane and hypnotic collections these places offer.

I can think of no better place to start than **City Lights Bookstore** (261 Columbus). Nestled in the bosom of North Beach, less than a shot glass throw from some of the most notorious beatnik dives, City Lights functions as both museum and breeding ground. Almost every literary classic of the human language is available there. Literature from around the world and around the block share shelf space in a kind of modern day Library of Alexandria which can devour weeks of time just in the act of browsing. The consignment area in the back has one of the best selections of small press/chapbook/zine/handmade object/literary journal publications available anywhere. The work in these things is uneven, but the pearls to be found in their pages are where the real future of literature will come from. And if it's the past you have a yen for, City Lights provides a choice which stretches back before Beowulf, earlier than Ovid, to Homer and beyond. Philosophy, art, history, and fiction, it's all there. An entire room upstairs is devoted to poetry only, offering one of the most comprehensive assortments in the U.S. All conveniently located across the street from Spec's and next door to Vesuvio's, two bars you can drink at and have an experience worthy of writing a poem about, or at least an adventure novel. I don't really have a religion, so City Lights is the closest thing I have to a church in this town. Ain't it time you did a little work on your soul?

Now let's shift channels quickly across town to the Haight, San Francisco's boho paradise of inebriation, piercing, tattoos, and general alternative brouhaha. Without a doubt, the best magazine store in this neighborhood and possibly the best in the city is **Naked Eye** (533 Haight). Without a doubt, stocking this store has been a labor of love, and it carries everything from *Time* and *Playboy* to slick top of the line fetish journals and magazines devoted to Asian Trash Cinema. A variety of locally and nationally produced zines share space with the rest. And if movies are your cup of tea, Naked Eye has a videotape selection that will make even the most jaded alternative hipper-than-thou bend over and hurl with delight. Midnight movies, splatter flicks, art loops, rockumentaries, foreign films, documentaries, Japanese monster movies, enough variety to pick every tooth in a culture vulture's beak.

Over five thousands titles. Five thousand! Do you know how many hours that is? And that's only if you can get past the magazines without spending every penny and wearing out your last synapse. There are books and movies at this store that I've never seen anyplace else. There's something here to document even the most obscure fringe.

Slide on up the hill to where Divisadero severs Haight Street and a short distance to your right is **Comix Experience** (305 Divisadero), a world class comic book franchise. Yeah, I know it's a comic store and not a book store, but comics are literature, so get used to it, okay? A healthy showing of undergrounds soak up shelf space and the miasmal aura of Todd McFarlane is remarkably dim. The people who work there are mellow and extremely intelligent. If you're looking for a title, ask them, they'd probably be familiar with it. A shimmering cornucopia of psychedelic colors and pictorial story lines make up the Comix Experience, there's more there than you could ever put on your tongue.

Up the hill, next to a shady courtyard on Haight Street, sits **Bound Together** (1369 Haight), the creme de la creme of anarchist bookstores. The outer walls of the collective display scrawled political slogans and a glowing mural. Inside is an anarchist's candy shop. For the armchair intellectual there are the collected works of great reformers and political thinkers throughout history, while the street fighter can peruse manuals on how to build bombs and molitov cocktails. Most of the Bound Together staff have a greater knowledge of politics, both contemporary and historical, than one could ever squeeze out of a poli-sci prof on any campus, and best of all, you won't have to listen to any intellectual ass kissing of the latest French darling of academia. Beliefs at this store are not molded by tenure, but they stock all the french philosophers anyway. Almost no idea is excluded from this place, no matter how controversial or unpopular. In fact there are so many voices available at Bound Together that even when the store is empty it seems deafening. On their shelves are voices you have been listening for all your life, voices that will change your life, voices that you agree with, disagree with; there will even be voices that annoy and outrage you. That's the point. Bound Together is one of the few bookstores in the country that is immune to the censor's amputation. As a result, the place is many limbed like Shiva, a deafening palette of clashing ideas, so many books, so many voices, a model of pure anarchy made from pictures and printed words, where the only thing that binds it all together is the collective's devotion to complete freedom and access to any and all information.

Now for information of a lighter headed nature one need only walk across the street to **Pipe Dreams** (1376 Haight). Pipe Dreams stocks some of the finest tobacco accessories and waterpipes west of Amsterdam. They also carry books. Besides tomes bursting with information for recreational growers, one can peruse rock fanzines, comics, and a mutant variety of underground publications. There's always something there guaranteed to light up every taste.

A short walk down to the eternal corner of Haight and Ashbury brings one to one of the oldest alternative bookstores in SF, **Great Expectations** (1512 Haight). Besides being your one-stop shop for Sixties and hippie related books and t-shirts, they also stock titles which span the ages. It's a small place, with books stacked up above your field of vision, giving it an atmosphere that is equal parts Edward Gorey and Human Be-In flashback. The cash register is so high up on a raised desk that when the clerk hands you your change he looks like a judge handing down a sentence. Charles Bukowski is still alive at Great Expectations and they usually have all his titles, as well as Burroughs, Kerouac, Gibson, and the rest of hipster required reading. For the best in literature and coffee table art and photography books, Great Expectations should live up to anybody's expectations.

A stone's throw away dwells **Anubis Warpus** (1525 Haight). It's one of a growing breed of places where you can buy a book about tattoos, bring it to the back of the store, and have their resident skin artist put your favorite design directly onto your flesh. Or if you just want to get a couple holes poked in your Johnson, they have facilities for that too. One can see a rainbow there just in the hair dyes that adorn the customers' heads. The fine selection of magazines and books take up an entire wall and radiate a fashionably bad attitude. Two tall bookcases are given over to erotic publications and the selection covers the distance from slick high end latex fashion catalogues down to xerox zines singing the praises of fat dykes and transsexuals. Comics, rock books, hip lit titles, and tomes of post modern theory flesh out this eclectic mix. They also sell clothes and t-shirts.

If you're a comic fan it's impossible to walk down Haight Street without being sucked into **Comic Relief** (1597 Haight) as if it were a black hole. That same gravitational force has amassed one of the largest and most eclectic comic collections in the country. Besides all the mainstream crap Comic Relief also stocks the entire Wow Cool catalog of mini-comics. You can find *Jar Of Fools* there, complete runs of Adrian Tomine's original *Optic Nerve* mini-comics, handmade Jim Woodring books. Their back issue selection is a collector's treasure trove. You'll find undergrounds like Rick Griffin's *Tales From The Tube* and Richard Corben's *Up From The Deep* that you just ain't going to find anyplace else. The employees there have a knowledge of the field that's bigger than the average Pentagon database. Got a question about an obscure gold or silver age title? Ask 'em. Even if they don't have the book they can probably give you directions on where to track it down. The store's connections branch out into that obscure underworld of completely obsessed collectors. Original artwork and small print run items show up in this place and you can't figure out how they found them. I'm talking the kind of stuff you'd have to bargain with the Freemasons to get. Rare Crumb, Giger, Dan Clowes, Peter Bagge, the list goes on and on. The best comic store I've seen in the world so far. What a relief to have places like Comic Relief in this town. Also check out their sister store in Berkeley, it's also a monument to sequential art.

Just a short hop down the street is **Booksmith** (1644 Haight). Booksmith has all the front list selection that a mainstream Barnes & Noble or Borders has, only the roots of their selection sink much deeper into the underground. Numerous small press offerings share shelf space with the classics. From street level literature to punk rock rants, these edges are where all the fun is. Say you want to buy a copy of Betty Page in Bondage trading cards or Peter Plate's latest novel, Booksmith has got them. They even branch out into fetish titles and deviant philosophy. The Art department boasts one of the best selections of full color hardcovers to be found in the city, while the magazine rack provides hours of fun.

Across the street and down a bit is **Austen Books** (1687 Haight), one of the better used bookstores in the city. Named after Jane Austen, they provide a rich collection of antiquarian rarities. A fascinating selection of pulp novels can kill hours of time just by looking at the lurid covers. Out of print classics of the Beatnik and earlier movements can be found here. But if you're looking for a how-to on piercing, like Research's *Modern Primitives*, they'd probably have it too. Though their general focus veers toward the intellectual realms of publishing there's enough pulp and trash fiction to keep any low brow well entertained.

That kind of finishes the Haight Street ramble, but if we move over to the Sunset, one finds another of San Francisco's premier book dens. **Green Apple Books** (506 Clement) has the musty dusty feel of the best old town libraries. There is a rustic and romantic atmosphere to the narrow alleys which wind between shelves which often reach up to the ceilings. There's something mysterious and magical about the character of the building itself, like it was just dropped here by a tornado from Kansas or something. Inside, it's all a crazed mix of the old and new. Out of print, used, and rare tomes are mixed in with the newest stuff. The front of the store assaults you with the hot off the press best sellers, but for my money the best finds are to be mined from the deeper aisles which wind like caves through two stories of rooms. Great old sci-fi, and detective noir pulps can be scored there. The art books section is one of the best, lots of discounted hardcovers and crisp color reproductions. They stock a great graphic novel section, and the store has a long history of being supportive of underground, small press, and local publishers. Don't go there if you're in a hurry. It's the kind of place you want to poke around in for ages.

Now let's shift gears rapidly over to the Mission District. **Modern Times** (888 Valencia), is one of those few places that take the idea of "diversity" seriously. Though they tend to steer towards the highbrow and intellectual, their selection is a monument to multiculturalism. So many races and civilizations seem to glow on its shelves. They have a rich philosophy section which seamlessly documents the span from ancient to contemporary. The great works of Eastern and Western civilization can be found there, as well as samplings from all other points of the compass. It's a selection that reminds one of the inherent dignity of the human condition. That's not to say that they're fuddy-duddy. If you need a quick manual on S/M or the latest stroke book from Masquerade Press, they'll probably have them too. The gay and lesbian section is sumptuous, the sci-fi and horror section divine. They even have a reading space in the back which frequently hosts some of the literary luminaries of our time. It's one of the few book peddlers out there where there truly is something for everyone.

Farley's (1315 18th St) is the last stop on our trip and that's a good thing, because their specialty is coffee. Take a walk up Potrero Hill, and kick back in their spacious and well lit ambiance. Their menu is a java junkie's dream and as you jump start your heart you can sample one of the best stocked magazine racks west of the Pecos. Farley's also carries books, but you won't find the best sellers there. Instead they specialize in local small press titles and obscure publications. A great place to score a copy of Danielle Willis's *Dogs In Lingerie* or Bucky Sinister's *King of the Roadkills*. The tables around you are often haunted by poets scribbling away in notebooks or artists filling sketchbooks.

Well, that just about does it for me. If you couldn't find that special book you were looking for by the end of this tour it's not San Francisco's fault. The last copy must have been burned by some Christian fanatic somewhere, or maybe Jesse Helms is hiding it in his bathroom. Long before the end of this tour any sane person able to read past the third grade level would have acquired more books than they could carry. Anyone literate who does the whole tour should be shipping stuff home bulk mail because it's too heavy for the plane. As for me, I'm heading back to my apartment to get some reading done.

PLEASURE AND PAIN, POKING AND PAINTING

BY BUCKY SINISTER

Do you really want to wear an "Alcatraz Swim Team" shirt when you get back home? No! The best San Francisco souvenirs are tattoos and piercings. Open up the yellow pages to "Tattooing." San Francisco has more tattoo shops per capita than anywhere else in the country. Getting a tattoo is a permanent and serious matter, so I'm not going to recommend any one place over another, so take a day out and judge for yourself.

If you must know, my absolute favorite place and a must visit place is **Tattoo City** (722 Columbus) in North Beach. It's run by Ed Hardy and always has top of the line artists who work in a variety of styles. Don't get people's names or political symbols tattooed on you. Ask to see examples of cover-up work they've done. Cover-up work is when people have a tattoo they don't like and get another over it that hides the original design. You will be handed a photo album full of swastikas turned into roses, and So-and-so Forever tats turned into snarling grim reapers.

The pictures on the wall are called "flash." These are popular images often done on people coming in on a whim: USMC bulldogs, skulls, snakes, panthers, skulls with snakes, etc. These are great, but don't think that's all you can get. Every artist does custom work. You can literally say, "I want a panther with a skull and snake tattoo on his arm sitting in an easy chair eating a bucket of Kentucky Fried Unicorn and reading a copy of Naked Lunch," and they'll do it.

Start small, and get it in a place where it's easily concealed. After having the tattoo around a year, you'll start to understand the concept of "permanent." Even if you're never going to run for Senate, a tattoo of a Tasmanian Devil smoking a joint will keep you from getting a minimum wage gig at Toys 'R' Us if it's in a highly visible place, like your neck.

For full body piercing, my best recommendations are **Gauntlet** (2377 Market) and **Body Manipulations** (3234 16th St). Check out each one, check out others listed, and see which one you feel comfortable with. Talk to the piercers, they're generally very nice people who are used to dealing with scared first timers.

Certain piercings will make walking difficult, specifically the 'guiche' (between your butthole and whatever's in front of it); the 'hafada' (scrotum); labia and penis piercings, etc. So if you're planning on getting it south of the border, bring loose clothes with you. Healing time can be anywhere from two weeks to two months, depending on the piercing.

Piercings, if the jewelry is taken out, will close up. If you don't like your nose ring in a few months, no biggie. For tattoos, all I can say is, the listing right under "Tattooing" in the Yellow Pages is "Tattoo Removal."

PASSIONATE DISTRACTIONS

KINKY SAN FRANCISCO

BY DAMIANA ZERO

One of San Francisco's most notable aspects is the kink factor, wherein anyone can indulge in their wildest fantasies (well, most of 'em anyway) and there are plenty of resources available for both novice and experienced connoisseurs of sex beyond the missionary position.

If you're into ogling women, you can pay top dollar and join the Japanese businessmen at the **O'Farrell Theater** (895 O'Farrell), or for a less hefty cover charge, check out Danielle Willis' erotic vampire act at the **New Century Theater** (816 Larkin). Or visit the women owned and operated **Lusty Lady** (1033 Kearny), which promotes itself as "clean, safe and fun."

Their entertaining ads run weekly in S.F.'s alternative free papers, seeking "responsible, sensual women" including "students, artists, and 9-5 gals with a wild side." Think about it, all you downtown receptionists and secretaries, what could be better than running into your gross, sleazy boss while you're stark naked in a strip joint?

If you're into ogling men, check out the **Campus Theater** (220 Jones), **Nob Hill Cinema** (729 Bush), or the **Tea Room Theater** (145 Eddy), which all offer a variety of performances or all-male films.

If you're into printed matter, **The Magazine** (731 Larkin) offers all sorts of vintage and contemporary porn (gay, straight, specialty). **Don's of Sixth Street** (111 6th St) will buy your used porn, as long as the pages aren't stuck together. **Good Vibrations** (1210 Valencia) is the fabulous sex shop owned by women and created specifically for women, though they welcome men, too. It is home to a variety of gay and straight porn and erotica, sex toys, and sex information.

Essential to the knowledgeable and the curious is the awesome weekly newsmagazine, *The Spectator*, available from newspaper vending machines strewn nearby BART stations and along Market Street. *The Spectator* has listings of events, including S/M parties, swing parties for couples, publication parties, art openings, and just about everything connected with the fetish and kink underground. *The Spectator* has articles penned by talented writers including Carol Queen, Pat Califia, and lots more. There is also extensive advertising throughout, including private dungeon rentals. If you're looking to rent a dungeon, try

Castlebar (552-2100), optional dominatrix extra.

If you're a neophyte on the B&D (bondage and discipline) and S/M (sadomasochism) scene and just want to check out some action without necessarily participating, visit clubs like **Bondage-A-Go-Go** (Wednesday nights) or **Ritual** (Saturday nights) at Trocadero Transfer (520 4th St). Don't miss the **Folsom Street Fair**, an annual event on one of the last Sundays in September, in which unusual passion fans of all persuasions parade around in the sunshine in their finest leather and latex gear, or in very little gear at all. At this year's event, a charity spank raised $3000, as volunteers paid a buck to get lashed by a sweet young thing.

For women, men, and couples interested in B&D and S/M, there are classes and seminars offered by **QSM** (550-7776), a highly respected S/M school located in San Francisco, which offers a plethora of demonstrations and classes, including 'Rope Bondage That's Safe and Secure', and 'Vaginal Fisting: Learn To Do It Right', taught by experts.

Queer sex clubs are still around. The **1808 Club** (1808 Market), and **Eros** (2051 Market) offer warm, safe settings for fulfilling fantasies of anonymous torrid sex. Condoms are provided on the house.

For stylish apparel, visit **Stormy Leather** (1158 Howard), which has a great assortment of leather and latex for women of all sizes (and men, too). Guys (and gals) can get their gear at **Mr. S Leather** (310 7th St). If you're into crossdressing, try **Piedmont** (1452 Haight), highly recommended for friendly service, a great assortment of feather boas, and all the necessary accoutrements for changing one's look genderwise.

Also check out the **Foxy Lady Boutique** (2644 Mission), which features shoes in sizes 3-15, wigs, lingerie, feathers, rhinestones and more. **McB's Shoes** (715 Market) offers large size women's shoes for all you Bigfoot types looking for some decent heels.

To celebrate the new you, order an explicit and delicious cake from the **Cake Gallery** (290 9th St; 861-CAKE). Their cakes are available in a wide range of body parts with suggestive decorations. Stop by and take a look at their photo album for ideas of just how exciting whipped cream cakes can be.

The wonderful world of kinky San Francisco is at your feet and this is just barely scratching the surface. To dig in deeply, just get started with any of the above scenes and you'll know why you came.

BACKDOORS & SIDE ALLEYS
QUEER SAN FRANCISCO

BY MILES LONG

Like a lot of homos fresh off the farm, magnetically drawn to Sodom-by-the-Bay, I thought that San Francisco was a monolithically homocentric paradise waiting for me to pluck the many pleasures found on its every street corner. Think again. While there's plenty to see and do for the discerning dyke or hankerin' homo, much of it isn't visible to the naked eye. Take the Castro, for instance. Please!

My first visit to this shrine for queer pilgrims was like bad sex: is that all there is to it? It all seemed so depressingly normal, almost quaint, full of overpriced shops and bland tourist traps. So much for my starry-eyed, media-driven fantasies about a round-the-clock Mardi Gras atmosphere ladled evenly across San Francisco's 46 square miles. The center of the gay universe was just another yuppified, inbred urban enclave, as far as I could tell. I was relieved to discover, over the next few months, that there was much more to gay life in San Francisco than the Castro. I also learned that the Castro had more to offer than my first disappointed inspection proved.

CLOTHING: PASSION FOR FASHION

Most of the Castro's clothing stores are full of tacky boring knockoff threads at hyper-inflated prices sold by retail clerks with more attitude than Diana Ross. A few others, however, are worth the effort. **NaNa** (2276 Market), with sister stores in L.A.; and New York, is terribly trendy but not terribly cheap. Good dirt never is. You'll dazzle (or at least fit right in) walking down the lean mean streets of S.F. or Hollywood. But bear in mind such fashionable frocks might look a wee bit silly in Pittsburgh or Tulsa. Across palm-lined Market Street is **Crossroads** (2231 Market, another branch at 1901 Fillmore), which sells cool as fuck, mostly secondhand, jobs at very reasonable prices. They also buy, trade, and take some items on consignment. So it's a good bartering spot for those of us who, with more taste than money, are constantly updating our wardrobes.

For cheap, trendy togs, most younger fags & dykes, like their straight counterparts, go to Haight Street or the Mission for thrift stores or second hand specialty shops. Always an experience. **Aardvarks** (1501 Haight) offers its own line of clothing, plus a plethora of used goods, especially denim, leather and brightly colored shirts & dresses. **Held Over** (1543 Haight) features a large selection of the usual fashion fare plus a lot of formal, forties, fifties and cowboy/girl drag. **Buffalo Exchange** (1555 Haight, 1800 Polk) buys, sells and trades the latest Gen X garments. **Wasteland** (1660 Haight) is the largest of the Haight Street shops, with a little more variety and a stronger hip hop flavor to its general selection. **Villains** (1672 Haight) is also heavily hip hop, with a generous selection of leather, tee shirts and shoes. Both Villains and Wasteland are popular with visiting and local rock stars. Wow. While none of the Haight Street stores are specifically gay, a sizable percentage of their employees and customers are of the fruity persuasion.

The Mission, which I like to think of as the Castro's less affluent, more exciting Latino cousin, offers better buying grounds for poor white trash like myself, looking for those elusive bargains in this, one of the more expensive cities in the galaxy. **Clothes Contact** (473 Valencia) offers clothes by the pound ($6, at last count). But the clerks often give you a discount if they think that's too much. **Community Thrift** (625 Valencia) is a gay-run charity, with most of its proceeds going to various gay and AIDS service organizations. Like most thrift stores, it sells everything besides clothing—housewares, music, furniture, bric-a-brac, books, videos, magazines, electronics. And like most thrift stores, it's really hit or miss what you find. Some days, it could be a great pair of boots for $7. Other days, nada. **The Salvation Army** (1509 Valencia,

1185 Sutter) is a large, disorganized jungle of clothing and furniture, often worth the effort if you have the time to sift through their vast melange. I once completely outfitted myself for a wedding at this store for under $25. And I was among the nattier dressers to this august occasion, I might add. Rounding out the Mission cheapies is **Thrift Town** (2101 Mission), among the largest secondhand emporia around these parts. Sadly, like many such shops in a town as trendy as ours, it often seems as if it has been picked clean, offering items that your grandmother probably wore five years ago. The best thing about Thrift Town is that they're constantly having sales to celebrate obscure holidays, such as Arbor Day or National Secretaries' Week. It's good to know that the silver lamé blouse you just bought is 30% off because George Washington & Abraham Lincoln both happened to be born in February. I love America!

Worn Out West (582 Castro) is the store for those of us who get a kick outta walking in shitkickers and cowboy drag. Among the leather set, **Stormy Leather** (1158 Howard) is popular among the younger crowd. Other homo leather stores include **A Taste of Leather** (317 10th St) and **Mr. S Leather** (310 7th St).

DRINK & BE MERRY

For better or worse, bars are the center of gay culture. Like churches in the black community, they are social and political magnets. And while all the old-timers claim it ain't like it used to be, there are still more choices in S.F. than anywhere between here & the West Village or West Hollywood. **The Detour** (2348 Market) is a favorite neighborhood hangout in the

Castro. With the cheapest beer, the darkest, tiniest interior, and the loudest music, it's bound to be interesting. Across the street is **The Cafe** (Market & 17th), still often referred to by its former name, Cafe San Marcos. This used to be considered the only women's bar in the Castro. And it was a good place for men to go who wanted to get away from the cruisey, hyper-male atmosphere in other local watering/glory holes. Unfortunately, word got out. Now, long, mostly male lines form outside on weekend nights, and the clientele seem to be 80% pushy, horny men. The last time I went there, it felt like a frat party. **The Mint** (1942 Market) is a cute karaoke bar, which attracts a diverse crowd, often drunk before they even arrive. Sadly enough, most of the rest of the Castro bars don't even rate this high. They're all scary, tacky, slop troughs full of sweater queens and the usual slew of gay desperadoes and alcoholics. **The Pendulum** (4146 18th St) could fit into this category, except that it is cheaper than most bars in the neighborhood, and is the only black gay bar that I know of in S.F. Its clientele is composed of near equal numbers of African-American men and their admirers.

Since this is a very cosmopolitan and racially diverse city, there are other gay bars which cater to different ethnic groups. **Esta Noche** (3079 16th St) is famous for its Latino drag queens and strippers. It is rather small and seedy, and always packed. It can be quite fun. **The N Touch** (1548 Polk), located in the heart of one of the oldest gay neighborhoods in the country, is a gathering place for Asian men and their admirers. You know how us white men love to colonize. It offers karaoke and male strippers on various nights throughout the week. Not far away is **The Motherlode** (1002 Post), an infamous drag hangout that's been packin' em in for years.

If you like the rugged type, then head south, South of Market that is. **The Eagle** (Harrison & 12th) has a real outdoorsy feel, with lots of biker & leather types lurking about. Every Sunday afternoon is an $8 beer bust. Beats the hell out of going to the park, eh? Down the street is **The Lone Star** (1354 Harrison), a rough macho kind of place with peanut shells strewn on the floor, and men swilling beer & talking loudly to one another. Across the street is **The Stud** (399 9th St), a legendary SF bar which has seen better days. Wednesday is $1 beer night (very popular), and other nights offer various club adventures.

Food: Eat Me

Let's face it, after clothes & booze, there's nothing a self-respecting homo would want to waste his hard-earned money on besides food. And why not?! It's one of life's few reliable pleasures. In the town that knows how (to cook, that is), finding decent grub is no problem. I don't know about you, but when I shell out my shekels for someone else's food, I want a lot of bang for my buck. **La Mediterranee** (288 Noe, also at 2210 Fillmore) serves up Middle Eastern food to a mostly homo crowd. For dinner, come early (before 7 p.m.). The place is rather tiny and fills up fast. **Amazing Grace** (216 Church) is sort of an earthy crunchy cafeteria famous for its vegetarian sandwiches. **Hamburger Mary's** (1582 Folsom), with its funky decor and employees, proximity to nightclubs, and late night hours, has been a perennial favorite of San Francisco's gay & lesbian community. But the prices are steep for their rather prosaic fare. Burger, fries, salad and a drink can run $12-15, an amount which used to feed me for a week when I was in school. Being the most nocturnal of creatures, queers dominate the late night food biz in SF, particularly in the center of town. **The Bagdad Cafe** (2295 Market), **Orphan Andy's** (3991 17th St), and **Sparky's** (242 Church) are all relatively inexpensive (if uninspiring) all night restaurants in the Castro-Upper Market area, frequented by fags & dykes of all stripes. **Hot & Hunky** (4039 18th St) is sort of like a queer Burger King. I like to think of eating there as a metaphor for much of gay sex: quick, easy, cheap, and mostly pain- and guilt-free.

CLUBS: DANCING QUEENS

If there's one thing we queers are good at besides hairstyling, floral arranging, pet grooming & home decorating, it's shaking our thangs. Lots of the aforementioned bars offer dancing. But sometimes, you want the total club experience. You know: bitchy door thing; indifferent coat check wench; slow as molasses, moronic bartender; sadistic security personnel; and dumb as clams DJs playing the same annoying music all night long. Gee, I wonder why people do a lot of drugs in clubs? To get over the intense boredom most of these places generate, I would guess.

Don't mind me & my crabby rantings. There's plenty o' fun to be had for those willing to look. Bear in mind there's a high turnover in clubland. The names

I write of here and now will more than likely change within a few months. The venues generally stay the same. So the important things to remember are the addresses. It seems as if about a half dozen or so spaces are used over and over for most of these ventures. A bit of advice: check out the record & clothing stores in the Castro for "invitation" cards to bars, clubs & parties. Most offer discounts on admission or even free admission before a certain hour.

The week starts out slow, as everyone is still catching their breath from the weekend, coming down from their chemically enhanced fun. Mondays offers Jazit Up at the **Cat's Grill** (1190 Folsom). The music is mostly funk & acid jazz, the crowd is racially mixed, mostly straight, but usually quite friendly. The cover charge is in the $3-$5 range. Tuesdays presents Come Unity (**1015 Folsom**), with a mixed (boy/girl, gay/straight) young, ravey crowd. This one has been going on for years now, one of the rare exceptions to the general rule of a club's short lifespan. Also on Tuesdays is Klubstitute (at The Stud, 9th & Harrison), a very offbeat homo cabaret, featuring lots of drag & local color. This one is constantly changing venues and nights. By the time you read this, it could be coming soon to a theater near you. The cover charge is usually $5.

On Wednesday, Faster Pussycat, a mostly dyke thang, purrs along at the **CW Saloon** (911 Folsom). Thursday gives us **Lift** (55 Natoma), which is relatively small & intimate, and quite queer. **The Box** (3rd & Harrison) is a big loud high energy disco with lots of cute boys and girls of all races. The cleancut crowd always seems to be having fun at this one. They seem downright wholesome by this town's standards. An antidote to all this sweaty cheer on Thursdays is Junk, at The Stud, a dyke club which attracts the modern primitive pierced & shaved crowd. The music ranges from punk to kitschy oldies. The cover is an affordable $3.

The End Up (6th & Harrison) is another stalwart venue for queer clubdom. Fridays features Madhouse (mostly boys, all queer, quite crowded, $5 cover). Saturdays is The Girl Spot (a lesbo lair, same cover price), and Sundays is T-Dance, starting at 6 a.m. for those restless souls of all genders & persuasions who just can't stop moving, shaking off a weekend of drugs and debauchery.

Saturday is obviously the big enchilada of club nights. Besides The Girl Spot, there is Spread (1015 Folsom), with four dance floors and lots of attitude. The cover is $10. **Club Universe** (177 Townsend) is currently club bunny heaven with lots of perfect, sweaty, half naked bodies gyrating and grinding to that incessant bass beat that gay boys seem partial to. You'll pay $10 to be part of the magic here as well. **Megatripolis** (4th & Harrison) is a hallucinogen-inspired club venture that is single-handedly trying to resuscitate the long dying local rave scene and bring it back to a semblance of its roots. I went on opening night and had a swell time. Of course it helped that it was free, I did lots of drugs, and knew a bartender. The crowd is very mixed with lots of British accents, cute hippies of all persuasions, and a lot of the true weirdos you tend to see if you go out enough in San Francisco.

The vibe is very cool & peaceful. And the cover charge, sustaining the Saturday night racket, is $10.

On Sundays, Jesus comes to the CW Saloon at 911 Folsom. It's sort of the opposite of Megatripolis. Billing itself as a "niteclub for faggots, dykes & freaks," wear leather or rubber, or you'll feel out of place. Jesus has made a name for itself with its piercing/B & D/S & M ritual performances, many of which are not for the faint of heart or weak of stomach. The cover is $5. Come early, come often.

SEX

It is said that San Francisco is recession-proof because our main industries are food and sex. And there are a lot of hungry people out there, no? What to do when you've got a hankerin' for a hunk o' beef? Never fear. Crack your cat o' nine tails in this town and you're bound to graze some flesh peddler.

For gay men seeking printed material of prurient interest, there's **Jaguar Books** (4057 18th St) in the heart of the Castro, specializing in magazines, calendars & sex toys. **Le Salon** (1124 Polk), a famous purveyor of male porn, offers a large selection of videos (some of it of the vintage '70s variety), and magazines (including European smut). **The Magazine** (920 Larkin) offers all sorts of old porn (gay, straight, specialty) dating back to the '50s. If you want in the flesh action, check out the **Campus Theater** (220 Jones), **Nob Hill Cinema** (729 Bush), or the **Tea Room Theater** (145 Eddy), which all offer a variety of performances, either live strip or jack off shows, appearances by today's bigger porn stars or all-male fuck flicks. **Good Vibrations**

(1210 Valencia) is the infamous sex shop by women, for women, and mostly about women. Unlike some male-dominated establishments of this nature, however, the opposite gender is certainly welcome here. It is home to a variety of sex toys, gay & straight porn & erotica, and sex information.

For those seeking the comfort of strangers in a strange town, sex clubs are making a comeback now that we've entered the second decade of AIDS. The **1808 Club** (1808 Market), and **Eros** (2051 Market) provide warm safe settings for cheap torrid sex with that special someone you'll never see again.

For those who want their carnal thrills al fresco, San Francisco provides a cornucopia of outdoor pickup spots. **Collingwood Park** (19th St & Collingwood, one block west of Castro) is synonymous with gay male sex. One recent warm evening when I happened to be strolling by en route to an indoor assignation (honest!), I witnessed scores of leering men of all ages, shapes and sizes, seeking to slake their lonely thirsts after one of those rare hot days. **Dolores Park** (between 18th & 20th Sts, Dolores & Church) is another infamous cruising spot. The southwest corner, with its gorgeous view of downtown, is the gayer section. The lower sections along 18th Street are dominated by Latino immigrant drug dealers. I've never experienced any difficulties in this park, but it is a notorious flashpoint for fagbashings. The conflicts arise because of a lack of communication, partly due to the language barrier. The dealers tend to be young, often handsome men, almost all of them straight, with a limited grasp of English. They seem friendly but furtive, offering their illicit wares. Some cruising queen could easily mistake their solicitations for sexual advances. Hence the misunderstandings with sometimes violent consequences.

Buena Vista Park (Haight & Baker) and **Corona Heights** (Roosevelt & 16th St, one block west of Castro) are neighboring hills, the yin & yang of gay cruising spots. Buena Vista is leafy & lush, a sumptuous, steep climb several hundred feet up above Haight Street, with a panoramic view of the Pacific Ocean, Golden Gate Bridge, downtown & the bay. You'll work those leg muscles as you view the male fauna in his predatory mode. Buena Vistans consist mostly of men over 35 with mustaches, walking their dogs (a universally popular ruse among cruisers). Corona Heights, just a block away, is smaller, but more rugged, a barren, stark outcropping of stone overlooking the gay center of town. The crowd here tends to be younger and more adventurous. You have to be to make the sometimes treacherous ascent to the top.

South of Market, San Francisco's clubland, with its density of male dominated leather and sex bars, is home to two famous public sex alleys. **Dore Alley** (between Howard & Folsom, 9th & 10th) has its own S & M oriented summer fair. **Ringold Alley** (between Folsom & Harrison, 8th & 9th) is more legend than fact at this point. Both of these places, victims of changing times, police crackdowns, AIDS, neighborhood complaints, etc., probably saw more action in years past.

Polk Street, the old heart of gay San Francisco, is now home to frightened immigrants and teenage hustlers. With lots of gay bars and sex shops, it is a magnet for troubled young runaways and the men who are attracted to them. This is not so much a pickup spot as a flesh market. Expect to pay for this tender veal. Other famous cruising spots include JFK Drive in Golden Gate Park, near Ocean Beach (automobile-oriented, lots of older, married types), Land's End, above Cliff House (a nocturnal phenomenon, can be dangerous), and Baker Beach, in the Presidio (the north end is clothing optional and heavily gay).

ALL THE WORLD'S A STAGE

There are a variety of theaters and performance spaces for homolesbos in San Francisco. Some are queer-specific. Others are just queer-friendly. For movie houses, the obvious choice is the **Castro Theater** (429 Castro), the grand old dowager of old style theaters, with an 80 foot ceiling, a giant chandelier, a wurlitzer & real live piano player to go along with it, that ascend and descend on a circular platform to and from the orchestra pit. The Castro Theater is home base for the San Francisco Gay & Lesbian Film Festival every June. The **Roxie Cinema** (3117 16th St) is another venue for the Film Festival. While the Castro shows more classics loved by gay audiences (*All About Eve*, *Valley of the Dolls*), and a lot of queer cinema, the Roxie tends to show film noir, violent action flicks and more experimental independent films.

For performances geared toward gay & lesbian audiences, **Josie's Cabaret & Juice Joint** (3583 16th St) is considered de riguer for big name touring gay acts—comedy, music, one person shows—all make the playbill here. **Theatre Rhinoceros** (2926 16th St) is a homo-run playhouse that presents original performances, often written and featuring local queer talent. It always seems to be in financial limbo, and its future at this date is uncertain. Across the street is the **Victoria Theater** (2961 16th St), which is open sporadically, offering its fair share of queer plays, cabaret acts & musical reviews. **Komotion** (2779 16th St) is another struggling performance & ideas collective that offers an alternative space for noncommercial music and other lively arts. While mostly straight, it is quite amenable to queers as well. **Epicenter** (475 Valencia) is the punk rock music collective in town, again mostly hetero, but with a strong queer presence. **21 Bernice** (that's the name, that's the address) is yet another alternative performance space presenting a variety of local acts ranging across the scales in genres and talent. It has become the home for the Sick & Twisted Players, a loose grouping of young, mostly queer performers, heavy into drag and camp, who do low budget spoofs of Generation X pop culture ephemera. Recent fare included *The Omen* & *The Towering Inferno*. **Red Dora's Bearded Lady** (4851 4th St) is a dyke hangout, a little cafe and performance space, with an outdoor patio. And yes, the proprietress indeed does have hair on her chin. **LunaSea** (2940 16th St) is a dyke performance space dishing up hot "switch" cabaret shows, amateur strip nights, and more. **SisterSpit** features women reading their poetry, prose, and doing performance art. It happens Sunday nights at the CoCo Club (139 8th St). While **Cafe du Nord** (2170 Market) is more of a bar (rather plush in the '20s speakeasy mode), and the crowd is mostly straight (though young and friendly and usually quite attractive), this place is pretty good and featuring local queer talent. Other spaces of interest for the gay & lesbian audience (dependent on the work of the moment) include **848 Divisadero** (a small, very alternative space), Artist's Television Access, or **ATA** (992 Valencia), **Theater Artaud** (450 Florida) a live/work/performance salon, and **Intersection for the Arts** (446 Valencia).

ART GALLERIES

This is familiar territory for many urban fags & dykes, especially in San Francisco, where everyone fancies themselves an artiste or performer of some sort. I'm not even going to deal with the big downtown galleries, where art is a commodity to be bought and sold by a tiny elite, or with stores that call themselves galleries, but in reality just sell softcore homoerotica. No, let's talk about the handful of places, some serious, some more whimsical, which actually trade in ideas and objects of interest to all sorts of queers. **Southern Exposure** (401 Alabama) is a neato alternative gallery with some impressive work at times, and enough clout to gain a measure of respectability (is that still a dirty word?). Other interesting galleries with a queer bent (to varying degrees) include **Morphos** (544 Hayes), **Architrave** (541 Hayes), and **New Langton Arts** (1246 Folsom). The **Keane Eyes Gallery** (651 Market), while not queer-oriented, is the home base for San Francisco's most famous painter, Margaret Keane. She, of course, is the progenitor of the large-eyed waifs, the fashionable icon of our youth-obsessed times.

MISCELLANY

A Different Light bookstore (489 Castro) is the Library of Congress for West Coast queer culture. It has it all, from coffee table volumes on supermodels to esoteric sociological studies. It is always crowded, morning, noon & night, and is the place to meet local or visiting gay & lesbian writers. **Old Wives' Tales** (1009 Valencia), which hosts readings and community events, is a major lesbian bookstore. **Bound Together** (1369 Haight) is a really cool anarchist book collective. They're very good with alternative queer material. Another favorite of mine is a cavernous used bookstore called **McDonald's** (48 Turk) which bills itself as "A Dirty, Poorly Lit Place For Books." What more could you want?

Leather Tongue Video (714 Valencia) has one of the best selections of way-out, hard to find videos. And it also sells comix and zines. Modern primitives seeking new metal thrills go to either **The Gauntlet** (2377 Market), which is very queer and quite expensive, or **Body Manipulations** (3234 16th St), which is more straight and a lot cheaper.

For caffeine cravers, **The Castro Cheesery** (427 Castro) offers some of the best prices in town for numerous exotic or prosaic blends of coffee beans or freshly ground. **Harvest Ranch Market** (2285 Market) is a popular shopping (and loitering) spot for fresh produce and other health-conscious organic fare.

TENDERLOIN BAR CRAWL

BY SPIKE

*****God drinks here ****Outstanding ***Worth the trip **O.K. if you're really thirsty *Skip it

Aging ex-service men tell humbling tales of wartime glory and postwar debauchery. Jaundiced, gin blossomed old drunks deliver bar stool sermons with time delayed bits of infinite wisdom. Somber jaded queens reminisce about youth, home, and Harvey Milk. Outside, there are violent shrieks and stifled cries, but Cookie welcomes you at the door with a handshake and a smile and the contrast is blinding. A columnist for a punk rock magazine reads one too many Beat novels and writes a pretentious intro.... wouldn't you?

95

The Tenderloin. Nothing tender about it, pal. It's fabled that it earned its name almost a century ago, when the police who patrolled this squalid area earned extra hazard pay. These cops could therefore afford the choicer cuts of meat, the tenderloins. These days, any shmoe with fifty bucks, a hard dick and a strong stomach can afford everything he needs and hours of it.

It is our city within a city. Sober, I have never felt entirely safe in the Tenderloin; but drink by drink the TL's womblike spell has put me in a fuckin' vice grip every time.

Mike, Jerry, Darv, Antoine, and I recently set out to dispel any and all current myths circulating about this misunderstood area. Later, dim recollections, photos, and Mike's extensive notes were our only reference point to document our departure from sanity into a nether world of smoky bars, neon signs, and transvestite prostitutes. And hopefully this will serve as an indispensable travel guide to both residents and visitors to our fair city.

Our first stop was the **Club Charleston** (10 6th St.★★★★★) and the bartender's name was Joe. Joe wouldn't and still won't accept tips under any circumstances. "Save it for when we raise the drink prices," he said. My hat goes off to this man.

Maybe it was the shape of the bar or its blinking neon sign, maybe the honest eyes and kind words of the bartender named Joe. Come to think of it though, it was probably the t-shirt pinned above the bar with EVERYTHING DIES emblazoned on the front. I don't know but I've grown very fond of this place in a few short visits, so I'd appreciate it if you took your dreadlocks and pierced lips somewhere else. You wouldn't understand.

Next was the **Peter Pan** (45 Turk/Full Bar★★★$_{1/2}$) which stands on the outskirts of the Tenderloin like a warning, "Come No Further — Go Back!" it seems to say like the sign at the entrance to the Black Forest in *The Wizard of Oz*. Any rational, sober person would take heed, turn tail and run, but for us, the sign seemed to read, "BEER! CHEAP! DANCING ELVES!" There was no turning back.

So in we went, thinking those graffiti laden doors would open straight into Never-Never Land. The place was almost deserted, save for some loser playing video poker, and a weathered queen perched at the furthermost corner of the bar. We approached this guy, and asked a few questions. "Name's Kit," he announced, "I run this place." Kit went on to give us a brief history of the bar, telling us everything about the place, most notably that it was one of the oldest gay bars in San Francisco. Funny, but at first glance I would have thought that this was one of the oldest punk clubs in the city. I would book a Johnny Thunders show here in a minute if he were still alive.

Halfway through our beers and games of pool we were ushered out because the bartender was called away to work at the Motherlode, which was extra busy that night. Drunk?... No, but we managed to muster up the courage to move up Turk Street into the **21 Club** (98 Turk/Full Bar★★) This place is fucking scary. There didn't seem to be any walls, just huge plexiglass windows which left bar patrons both visible and standing still, two very compromising positions in the 'Loin. Some of the eyesores in the bar included beefcake cop calendars for sale, surreal wood carvings, and thousands of backstage passes from the Warfield proudly plastered everywhere. At one point somebody belched and the whole bar cheered. Guys with buck knives in belt sheaths, and rockers of questionable sex and integrity drove us out and across the street into the **Club 65** (65 Taylor/Full Bar★★★★1/2) Wow... the contrast was overpowering. In fact there was an almost physical rush we felt entering from one of the most filthy, crime ridden streets in the city into a drunkard's paradise and the good graces of our host, Dale.

Upon entering we were greeted with a chorus of jeers from the locals at the end of the bar. "Uh-oh, here come the teeny-boppers," they shouted. At 23, I was the youngest of our group so this was pretty surprising. These guys must have been fucking ancient, gathering dust on barstools that probably had their names inscribed on the seats. After warning these dime store hecklers that "we've killed better men for less," I ordered a beer, put a couple of quarters in the pool table and got real loose. My opponent was a grizzled ex-con who muttered inaudible proverbs whenever I missed a shot. But I wasn't here to make new friends, so I quickly lost the game and joined Mike who was asking Dale about the place. Turns out a group of large Samoan semipro bowlers own the bar, and as if on cue these jokers in loud Hawaiian shirts and dress slacks burst in, from a bowling tournament I presume, and exclaimed "We're number one! We're number one!" Ex-cons, trophy wielding Samoans, and I thought I could feel a buzz creeping in. Well, I had work to do, so we bid a fond adieu to the old 65.

On to **Aunt Charlie's** (133 Turk/Full Bar★★★) How can you go wrong with a place that has a peach and pink interior? You get the impression that broken-down old queens that were exiled from the Castro and never made it on Polk Street end up here. Mike watched as two elderly gentlemen argued about who had a facelift and who didn't, but I didn't want to hear about it.

I stumbled upon the jukebox and entirely by accident found *Needle and the Spoon* by Skynyrd and *When I'm 64* from Sgt. Pepper. How could I have imagined how appropriate my musical selections would prove to be? Kit from the Peter Pan showed up wearing a new leather vest that said RAMROD in studs on the back, and generally ignored us. I know how to take a hint, and the **Coral Sea** (220 Turk★★★★★) was right down the street anyway. This is without a doubt the best bar in San Francisco. Red lights and tastefully displayed beer signs shone on spacious tables and semi-secluded booths along the wall to our right; and to our left, a fifty-foot rosewood bar stretched all the way back to the pool room. The wall-length mirror behind the bar was lovingly adorned with Christmas lights, happy hour specials, and liquor bottles, as well as witty framed proverbs about truth, alcohol, and credit here and there. Neither Cookie, the ex-Navy Admiral who opened the bar after the war, nor his beautiful wife, Betty, were present at the time of this particular visit, but old photos hanging by the door reminded us of their earlier hospitality. On hand though, were Beverly and Willie, two of the sweetest old foxes you could hope to meet. Beverly got us our drinks, and handed us all restroom tokens along with our change. I marveled at the classiness of that gesture and then decided to play myself a game of pool. While I was on the table, I vaguely heard somebody strike up a conversation with Mike, who was still at the bar. I soon forgot about it until...

"I think cars are a menace... They ought to be outlawed," I overheard Mike's new friend say. It seemed Mike had a few things to talk about, so I went back to improving my game. Soon, though, pool-fare lacking, I snuck over to see what this conversation was all about. The person admonishing Mike on the evils of automobiles was a bitter, middle-aged guy who trembled slightly when he spoke. Mike, being the publisher of Gearhead and all, tried unsuccessfully to defend car culture until he was out of breath. Mike's new buddy suddenly stared very seriously at him.

"You see, cars aren't the problem," he said. "It's people, and population control is the only answer." Beverly and Willie, looking increasingly uncomfortable at this point, cast their eyes sadly into space as if to say, "Not again, please, not again..."

"What do you propose?" Mike asked cheerfully.

"Mass sterilization, right across the board!"

Silence.

"Although I have never done it, I am capable of contaminating the water supply."

"At the reservoir?" Mike asked carefully

"No, at the water treatment plant, silly! You see, you take the..." He was really trembling now.

"Well, we gotta go man! But, uh, hey, great talkin'

to you. Maybe someday I'll introduce you to some of my friends."

"Bring a scientist, not a philosopher!" he urged, but we were already long gone to the **Kokpit** (301 Turk★★★★★). The name couldn't have been more appropriate. As we took a seat at the bar, Jesse, our bartender, leaned towards me and in a whispered voice confirmed that we were, in fact, "straight."

"Well, yeah" I muttered sheepishly.

"That's OK," whispered Jesse. "You guys look like fun."

Uh-oh.

I barely touched my beer before Dingy Don introduced himself to me as the longest reigning cowboy in San Francisco. "Oh, you mean in the gay rodeo," I said (my first big mistake).

"Jeez (hic) no... just around... you know, here and there."

"Oh." Boy, did I feel stupid, guess I set myself up for that one. Not wanting to pursue that conversation any further, I stared indifferently at the framed stained glass centerpiece behind the bar. KOK PIT — JOIN THE MADNESS, it read. Hmmm... tempting but...

"I'm very (hic) shy, you know." It was Dingy Don again, smiling like he wanted to hog tie me to a fence post. One of the two bitter old queens hunched over the end of the bar provided me with a much needed distraction.

"Jesse!... Jesse!" he screamed in drunken slurring lisps. "Another beer over here Jesse!" while his pal beside him stared despondently at the blue shag carpeting that lined the wall.

"You're cut off, Lance, stop it," Jesse responded (like he had heard it a million times). After sulking for about fifteen minutes, Lance reinstated his demands, "Jesse! Jesse!" I think Lance's shrieks will haunt me forever. "Another beer!" he wailed, undaunted by Jesse's blunt refusal. This went on and on for what seemed like hours until we left. Yes, I suppose theirs was a private hell, and I consider myself lucky to have caught even the briefest glimpse inside.

Oh yeah, I almost forgot my second big mistake. As my new friend, Dingy Don, barely stood up to stagger outside, I smiled politely and shook his hand (mistake). Cowboy Don planted his fat hairy kisser on mine and left it there for the longest ten seconds of my life. Afterwards, I took a deep breath and stoically finished my beer. I looked up to see Mike and Darv's mouths agape in disbelief. "Holy shit," they would have said if they could speak. "Holy fucking shit."

In keeping with this night of mind numbing contrasts, we decided to haul our asses from that pit of "koks" straight into that urban isle of whisky drinkin', potato eatin' macho misery: **Harrington's Pub** (460 Larkin★★★1/2). With tables lined up in the middle of the joint like lunch time at the Stuttering County Fair, this barely lit bar appealed strangely to my barely Irish sensibilities. An ill-tempered man behind the bar wearing an IRELAND t-shirt introduced himself. "Me name's Patty!"— oh god, here it comes— "What?...Paddy?" Mike asked innocently enough. "PATTY!!" our bartender bellowed. "Short fer Patrick!" After briefly lecturing Mike on Irish slurs and common responses, I ordered a whisky with a beer behind it, and quietly took stock in my surroundings. There wasn't much to distract me from my drink, so drink I did. But mid-beer I was interrupted.

"CLOSIN' TIME," shouted Paddy. What!? It wasn't even midnight! Patrick softened the blow by giving us all green drink chips, "Good fer a drink anytime–BUT NAY TONIGHT!" We got the picture and got up to leave. On our way out he invited us in for lunch. "WE GOT BOILED CABBAGE!" Aye.

The next place I've passed on my way home quite a few times, but never thought twice about actually entering. Anyhow, Jerry boldly led us through the swinging doors of the **Brown Jug Saloon** (496 Eddy/ Full Bar★★★★) We landed quite by accident at a birthday party, the likes of which I had never seen. The bash was being thrown for a woman who, incidentally, once propositioned me on the street. We found a spot at the bar, ordered $1.00 glasses of Miller, and watched in quiet awe as a drunken group of people tried unsuccessfully to form a straight conga line. This lasted less than a minute until one balding gimp in a nehru jacket broke away and danced spastically by the jukebox, eventually collapsing into the arms of the other revelers. Fuck, I didn't know whether to feel smug or jealous.

I could have been mistaken but all eyes in the bar seemed to be staring at us, and these were more than friendly stares. The party was over, and again we had work to do.

Come no further than **Jonell's** (401 Ellis/Full Bar- Strong cheap drinks!★★★★) for your last history lesson. A woman behind the bar wearing a Sturgis t-shirt enthusiastically beckoned us inside, so we sidled up to the bar and ordered our first round. The actual bar was set up like a sort of U-shaped feeding trough, which made for an interesting visual effect. John, one of the people hungrily 'feeding' there introduced himself. "This place was once classy, I made it classy." John chose Jerry for the obligatory ear-bending. See ya Jerry. I, on the other hand, moved over to the corner which was less crowded, so drinks could be more easily ordered. Already seated there was a British woman in her mid-70s wearing a lavish bright red outfit which, she later revealed, was of her own design. She spoke with an almost aristocratic—if somewhat slurred—English accent, and in a low scratchy scotch-soaked voice. My new friend Kathleen began to tell me stories from her life in Britain during the Second World War, pausing occasionally to pinch my cheeks and compliment my boyish looks. When I told her that my grandfather was a decorated General back then, some asshole sitting next to her suddenly said, "A General, huh?...What the hell happened to you?" I was caught off guard and didn't respond, so he went on with more war stories, this time from Vietnam. I had a war on either side of me.

Then suddenly, a pug-nosed drunk with a upturned baseball cap put me in a bear hug and kissed me on the cheek. "I'm a hobbies investigator," he boasted. "Wanna see my badge?" He flashed me a beat up old business card with a star and some writing on it, and then sat back down.

We sat for awhile with our new friends, and as the time flew by so did the whisky and beer, and I eventually found myself at a table with Mike, drunkenly reasserting dominance over my wife. "FROM NOW ON, I WEAR THE FUCKIN' PANTS AROUND HERE...GET IT?...ME!" Sorry, Katja.

Right in the middle of my soliloquy, Kathleen called me aside. "I want you to see how I live, young man," she said, asking me to escort her home. I was being hit on. I politely refused, explaining that I had work to do. She kissed me goodnight, stumbled and spilled Mike's beer right into his lap. Then, regaining her composure, she strode elegantly to the door.

Back at the bar, I tried to engage the Vietnam guy in some small talk, but he just scowled disgustedly at me.

"I know you're a hustler, you know you're a hustler, and any damn fool who takes you home better watch his wallet." I couldn't believe it! First, some cretinous cowboy kisses me with his eyes closed, then I'm branded a whore by a West Point dropout! So long Jonell's, I didn't even bother denying it.

Right across the street was our last stop, the **Cinnabar** (397 Ellis/Way Full Bar★★★). Things were getting pretty cloudy by now. The bartender's name was Paula, and after we told her what we had been up to, she told us that she had worked in almost every bar we had been in. Anytime anyone's name was mentioned in the context of alcohol, she would say, "He was totaled." So being that it was 1:30 a.m., that became the big word for the rest of the evening. Everyone in the place was either shooting pool for money or playing poker machines really hard. I think I did a little of both. One thing's for sure, I don't remember going off on Middle Eastern men, until Mike played a tape of me shouting obscenities in the men's room the next day.

Well, somehow we all made it home, and I slept for the next sixteen hours. I guess it's true what some people say, "The Good Lord always watches over drunks." Hey, where's my fuckin' hazard pay?

HOW TO BE A
MISSION SCENESTER

BY BUCKY SINISTER & SETH MALICE

Come pose with the best alternateens in the U.S.! The Mission is the hippest spot in town for 18 to 35-year-old scenesters. Not from San Francisco? No problem, no one else is either. Chances are you're going to run into that guy from high school who was drawing the Blue Oyster Cult symbol all over his notebook, but now he's got pattern baldness, short hair, and he's dressed as a swinging Dean Martin/Darren Stevens, and listens to the cool cocktail sounds of Martin Denny, Chet Atkins, and the Combustible Edisons. All the Mission you need to pose in is located on Valencia Street from 16th to 24th Streets, the hip strip, a Sesame Street for new arrivals. Occasionally you'll need to stray over to Mission Street itself. If you want to make the scene and not look like a tourist, follow these easy steps.

First, you've got to look the part. Hipper than any nightclub is **Community Thrift** (625 Valencia). On a Saturday or Sunday afternoon, it looks like you have to get your hand stamped to come in. This is the place to come and buy your cheap thread gear. For mere dollars, you can get decked out in one of several popular styles:

The Alternative Gas Station Attendant: Blue collar job clothes are cool! Dress like an employee of a place you'd never work, but be sure your tattoos show, you've got your facial piercings in full regalia, or dye your hair so no one would ever think that you might be for real.

The Eisenhower: Harken back to the days of Dwight D.! Guys, cut that hair; girls, get a pair of Far Side glasses, even if you don't need optical help. Guys should wear hats and jackets at all times.

FunkyRetroEveryEra: Adidas jogging suits, iron-on t-shirt designs, and suede Pumas. Girls, don't forget to look in child's medium for that baby doll t-shirt, and please don't forget barrettes, the more childish the better.

Other thrift/used clothing/vintage shops of note: **Captain Jack's** (866 Valencia), **Superthrift** (560 Valencia), and **Thrift Town** (2101 Mission). What's the difference between thrift store clothes and vintage clothing? Usually about twenty-five bucks.

If you really want to accessorize, be sure and stop

by the SPCA and pick up a pit bull or a rottweiler. This will complete any look.

Once you look like all the other individuals, it's time to go mingle with/ignore them. Early in the day, you can bet these joints are juking:

The Club (920 Valencia) coffeehouse: Get wired. The strongest coffee in town is the special Max's Blend, used by this and other cafes such as **Muddy Waters** (521 Valencia) and **Muddy's** (1304 Valencia). The Club, however, is located smack dab in the middle of the hip strip, right at 20th and Valencia.

The Chameleon (853 Valencia): This bar, also near 20th and Valencia, is open at ten a.m. and serves Max's Blend as well. They have espresso, too. The big bonus here is they serve a complimentary cigarette with every coffee drink ordered. Smokers, this is the last place in town to smoke inside while you sip your joe.

New Dawn (3174 16th St): It has the biggest mound of potatoes for $2.50, and is decorated like Pee Wee's playhouse. This also the place to show off who you slept with last night.

Mission Grounds (3170 16th St): This place has build-your-own crepes! Special bonus seats in the windows, so everybody going by can see who you're with and what you're wearing.

If you're having a bad hair day or you're trying to dodge the person you slept with last night, these places have great food but rank low on visibility points:

Pizza Pop (3274 21st St): Monstrous slices will keep you full. Live wild and order a calzone. They're fresh made here, unlike the "calzone roulette" game you'll play at all the cafes and corner stores, in which they have three kinds of calzones brought in at the beginning of the day, and you'll never know if they're beef and cheddar or spinach and mushroom until you bite into it.

Truly Mediterranean (3109 16th St): You'll never have falafel this good again in your life. The only place to go when you've got an eggplant craving.

Taqueria Cancun (2288 Mission): The best grilled steak is right here. That's carne asada (car-nay ah-sah-da) in your chihuahua-sized burritos, or on your torta, a delicious Mexican sandwich.

The 16th and Mission Cafeteria (2022 Mission): Big omelette breakfasts with coffee for $2.80? Why so cheap? Discounts for the atmosphere. Picture a bus terminal with a la carte dinners instead of candy machines.

Sit at these places as long as you can and act like you've done everything so much more than anybody that you're completely bored and burdened by the monotony of being fabulous. Never show up for breakfast before eleven. Noon or one is better, and two is the best. If you arrive too early, someone might think you have a job.

You've got a few hours to kill before the bars fill up, so do something to fit your mood. Swing by **Good Vibrations** (1210 Valencia) for a new butt plug or vibrator. Catch a movie or rent a video. The **Roxie Cinema** (3117 16th St) changes films daily, often times having two or three different films a night; it may be a Kim Novak tribute night, outtakes from the Simpsons, or Hong Kong action films. For renting videos, hit the **Leather Tongue Video** (714 Valencia). If caught in a conversation, remember: your favorite director is John Woo, your favorite actor is Harvey Keitel, and you love Blaxploitation flicks. Ask what they have in these categories, and regardless of what they tell you, just nod your head and say, "Seen it," after each title, with occasional "Loved it," here and there. Then pick up any movie with Dennis Hopper in it and say, "God, I haven't seen this in forever," and rent it.

Two record stores, both near 16th and Valencia, are of note. **Epicenter** (475 Valencia) is a punk rock run, all volunteer organization. If they don't have the punk rock record you're looking for, chances are the band has officially sold out: shaken hands with the Devil and signed to a major record label. Epicenter won't have any of these. Now you're off to the **16th Note** (3162 16th St), a new and used record store that has the Green Day album you've heard of.

San Francisco has a diverse music scene, with many venues and bands for all types of crowds. However, you're jaded, remember? You're so tired of hanging out at **Kilowatt** (3160 16th St) and seeing bands like J Church, or holding up the walls at the Chameleon while being bored by Jawbreaker. You saw all those bands when they were cool, you like their old stuff better, so tonight you're going to go out drinking! Besides, the only fashionable way to go see a band is to be on the guest list, and then you really better act bored and complain. By the way, when a band won't get you in for free anymore, that means they have definitely sold out.

The **Latin American Club** (3286 22nd St), which has nothing at all to do with Latin Americans, is the place to suck down your mixed drinks. If you don't have experience with this kind of drinking, just wait until you find out what the drink of the month is, (this will be the one that everyone is drinking but couldn't tell you what was in it mere weeks ago.) If in doubt, order a Cape Cod. This is also the place where you're most likely to see out-of-town bands getting plastered after the show. Do not, under any circumstances, let on that you like the band, but it's okay if you acknowledge the band's presence by slagging them to a neighbor. Example: "Oh, God, it's Evan Dando from that shitty band the Lemonheads. I hate them so much."

The Chameleon, where you might have gone for coffee, also has over twenty beers on tap that you've never heard of. Read a name off the list, and confidently order it like it was in your baby bottle. If someone asks you to play pool, refuse, but offer to play them a game of ping pong. There's a table downstairs.

Looking for a total dump? Park yourself on one of the gross couches at the **Uptown** (200 Capp). Don't sit on any of the patrons that have been parked on the faded sofas there for twenty years.

Feeling drained yet? Time to do some speed! Wait until you hit it off with the local riff raff, and just ask. Someone or their roommate has some. A quick sniff and the time flies to last call, and then you're kicked out of the bars and off to the night. Hopefully, you're on your way to a party, or someone's house to have some noncommittal but safe sex. If not, this neighborhood's weak on 24 hour places. **Magic Donuts** (2400 Mission) is open all night and has the best doughnuts in the city. Guys, if you didn't meet that magic woman, don't despair. At 17th and Capp, right outside the Uptown, prostitutes are at work all night and all day. Don't let the track marks and numerous scabs scare you. Handjobs are fairly safe.

At the end of the day, ask yourself: did I have fun? If so, sell off that return ticket and stay! Follow these directions lather/rinse/repeat style until you run out of funds. When you're completely broke, jobless, and homeless, but you look good, congratulations! You're a real live San Francisco hipster!

OTHER COOL MISSION STUFF

Anarchist **Emma Goldman** lived at 569 Dolores in 1916. **24th Street** is home to some really rad happenings. Check out **Latin Freeze** (3338 24th St) where amazing frozen fruit bars in traditional and exotic flavors are sold — tamarind is one of my favorites. **Balmy Alley** is a block-long Latino muralfest, an unrivalled display of public, community-based art. U2 shot one of their videos there a while ago. **Clarion Alley** (between Mission & Valencia) has murals by some of SF's best-loved '90s underground comix artists like Matso, Keith Knight, and Greta Snyder. Buy good luck candles and supplies for casting magic spells at **Botanica Yoruba** (998 Valencia). Fresh, handmade tortillas are served daily (and also sold by the dozen) at **Casa Sanchez** (2778 24th St)

MISSION SCENESTER ZONE

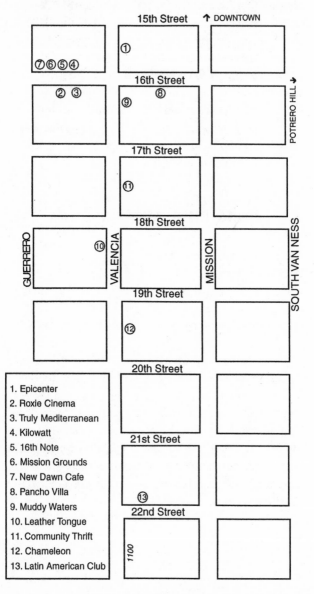

1. Epicenter
2. Roxie Cinema
3. Truly Mediterranean
4. Kilowatt
5. 16th Note
6. Mission Grounds
7. New Dawn Cafe
8. Pancho Villa
9. Muddy Waters
10. Leather Tongue
11. Community Thrift
12. Chameleon
13. Latin American Club

114

HAIGHT ASHBURY

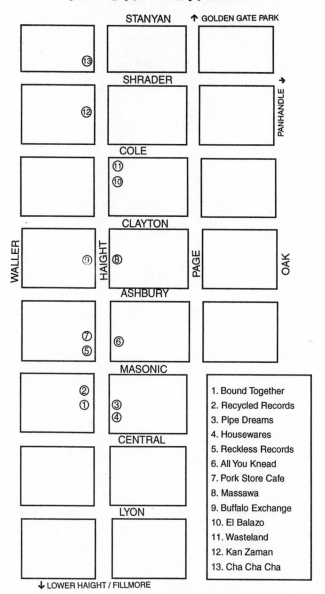

STANYAN

↑ GOLDEN GATE PARK

⑬

SHRADER

⑫

→ PANHANDLE

COLE

⑪
⑩

CLAYTON

WALLER
HAIGHT
PAGE
OAK

⑨
⑧

ASHBURY

⑦
⑤
⑥

MASONIC

②
①
③
④

CENTRAL

LYON

1. Bound Together
2. Recycled Records
3. Pipe Dreams
4. Housewares
5. Reckless Records
6. All You Knead
7. Pork Store Cafe
8. Massawa
9. Buffalo Exchange
10. El Balazo
11. Wasteland
12. Kan Zaman
13. Cha Cha Cha

↓ LOWER HAIGHT / FILLMORE

115

HAIGHTIN' IT

BY PATRICK HUGHES

For the last seven years, I've lived above Bound Together Books, the anarchist collective bookstore on Haight Street. I've lived in just about every room in this house. I moved here because Haight Street reminded me of St. Mark's Place in New York, which is where I'm from. Yeah, there a lot of street people asking for spare change but it doesn't bother me. I like the hustle and bustle, and the fact that everything you could ever want is right outside your door.

Like, say you want breakfast. **All You Knead** (1466 Haight) has been around since the '60s, and is still serving up $1.99 breakfast specials. **Dish** (Haight & Masonic) is good, a little upscale. The **Pork Store**

Cafe (1451 Haight) is really great. I often cruise down to the Lower Haight for breakfast, to the **Studio Cafe** (248 Fillmore). It doesn't have the obscene crowds like some of the other places in the neighborhood, like **Kate's Kitchen** (471 Haight) or **Spaghetti Western** (576 Haight), which both do a good breakfast if you don't mind standing in line.

If you have family or friends coming in from out of town, take them over to **Cha Cha Cha** (1805 Haight) for a meal. The decor is really fun Mexican iconography, based on Day of the Dead and Cinco De Mayo artwork, and the staff is friendly. They serve tapas, so you order a whole bunch of little dishes and split them. Get a big pitcher of sangria. It's not totally cheap but it's not totally expensive either. Great for a splurge.

If you're really broke, you can get a giant food bomb called Bob's Burrito at **El Balazo** (1654 Haight). They also have great veggie tacos for $1.25. **Massawa** (1538 Haight) is fun for a group of pals — they serve Ethiopian food, no forks, fingers only. The pizza in San Francisco can't compare to New York's but slices at **Cybelle**'s (1535 Haight) are $2. If you desperately need to eat green things, the salads at the **People's Cafe** (1419 Haight) will help. They also have giant slabs of fresh bread and good soups for when the fog rolls in early.

Shops in the Haight come and go all the time. When I first moved here, there was a cookie shop phenomenon. Every other store was a cookie/croissant/muffin place. And then it became a used clothing mecca, which seems to have had a certain amount of longevity, with stores like **Buffalo Exchange** (1555

Haight) and **Wasteland** (1660 Haight), which seem to specialize in retro–'70s wear, but frankly I'm not into that stuff, so you'll have to check it out for yourself. Certain clothing stores like **Villains** (1672 Haight) feature clubwear, while **Backseat Betty** (1590 Haight) has boudoir naughty clothes that are outrageously expensive.

Headshops? They're synonymous with Haight Street. **Pipe Dreams** (1376 Haight) has cheap cigarettes, and every other kind of smoking accessory. Also a good source for whip-its. If you're interested in rave culture, there are a couple places: **Housewares** (1322 Haight) and **Behind The Post Office** (1504 Haight). They've got tapes, clothing, and flyers for where the raves are happening.

There are great bookstores and comicbook shops on Haight Street, but Jon Longhi goes into detail about 'em in his chapter.

Record shops on Haight Street are the best in the city. **Rough Trade** has all the latest alterna-nation releases, both new and used. Also really good for indy imports, and they sell advance tickets for some of the independent clubs in town. [Ed. note: Rough Trade recently relocated to 695 3rd St & Townsend; 543-7091.] **Recycled Records** (1377 Haight) has the vinyl. **Reckless Records** (1401 Haight) has new and used, a good selection of goth, industrial, pop. **Gabardine's** (342 Divisadero) is more eclectic, geared toward the UK dance scene, with a great selection of dub, jungle, etc. Great place for rare imports.

As far as nightlife, I've always enjoyed going to the **Gold Cane** (1569 Haight). It's got a really wonderful neighborhood bar ambiance. On the weekends, it can get kind of crowded with suburban types, but otherwise it's okay. **The Deluxe** (1511 Haight) is also fine during the week, but they charge at the door on the weekends. Another place I like is **Trax** (1437 Haight), which is a low-key, mostly queer bar. They've got a great pool table. Then there's **Nightbreak** (1821 Haight), which is forever changing owners. They have live music but the whole place is dark and dingy, and smells like stale beer, stale cigarettes, and stale music. **Murio's Trophy Room** (1811 Haight) is down the street and is reminiscent of a fratboy hangout. I've always gotten along fairly well with Bruno, who's owned the **Persian Aub Zam Zam** (1633 Haight) for like 50 years. He's infamous for throwing people out if he doesn't like you, but he does make a kick-ass martini. It's kind of a high visibility place so it's just not a great place to hang out with your friends. **Kan Zaman** (1973 Haight) serves warm wine and middle eastern food, and you can smoke apple tobacco in a hookah while watching belly dancers.

In the Lower Haight, I can usually be found at **Toronado** (547 Haight), which has some really decent Happy Hour specials, a wide selection of beer on tap. It's a good place to watch a game on TV without being in a crowded, gross sportsbar. **Mad Dog In The Fog** (530 Haight) is a good place for pints, but the seating is tough. It gets really crowded. I like the **Armadillo** (200 Fillmore), which is down Fillmore near Waller. **The Top** (424 Haight) is also a worthwhile drinking establishment. **Nickie's Barbecue** (460 Haight) is always a great place to go dancing with pals.

The **Horse Shoe** (566 Haight) is a cafe full of colorful characters, sort of sleazy yet fascinating, one of the best people-watching spots in the city. The **Cafe International** (508 Haight) is very sincere, full of tortured artists. On Divisadero and Hayes is the **Bean Bag** (601 Divisadero) — the staff is very friendly and it's a mellow place to have coffee without having to deal with a major fashion show. In the upper Haight is the **Coffee Zone** (1409 Haight), where you'll observe all kinds of aberrant behavior and outfits, but they do pour a cup of coffee that is best described as astringent. After having a morning dose of their coffee, I often head down the street to **Haight Street Natural Foods** (1621 Haight) for a fresh cup of wheatgrass juice. They're not cheap but better than shlepping over to **Real Foods** (1023 Stanyan).

There's never a dull moment in the Haight. The people-watching is great because of the juxtaposition of everyone from demure tourists who take pictures of everything, to Gap-wearing suburban types, to the really flipped-out street scene which embraces punks, hippies, Deadheads, old-time drunks, and what not. The Haight's relatively safe during the day because there are so many people around, but you have to watch yourself on the street after dark. Buying drugs from strangers is never a great idea, but just for your information, "buds" refers to marijuana and "doses" refers to LSD.

HISTORICAL HAIGHT ASHBURY

Besides being one of the people-watching capitols of the world, the Haight Ashbury is steeped in rock'n'roll history. For the thrill of it, park your butt on the very steps that legends like Jimi Hendrix once trod. But don't be surprised if the current owners kick your butt off their property.

112 Lyon: Janis Joplin's house.

142 Central: Jimi Hendrix lived here.

710 Ashbury: The Grateful Dead house.

130 Delmar: Where the Jefferson Airplane lived before fame and fortune bought them a mansion at 2400 Fulton.

636 Cole: House of Manson (where Charlie, Squeaky, and the rest of the gang lived before heading south to LA).

318 Parnassus: Gonzo journalist Hunter S. Thompson lived here while writing *Hell's Angels*.

2500 block of Geary: Richard Brautigan lived here in the '60s, before he moved north to Bolinas.

Courtney Love used to live in the lower Haight and rumor has it after a recent Hole show at the Fillmore Auditorium, she jumped on a 22-Fillmore bus and inebriatedly announced as the bus crossed Hayes Street, "I used to live right there!"

THERE'S NO BEACH IN NORTH BEACH

BY JENNIFER JOSEPH

Okay, so I retired to North Beach at the age of 22. By that time I had lived in three different places in the Haight and in a big house in Berkeley with nine people, and frankly, after driving across America six times in four years, and divvying up my time between SF, NY, and Ohio, I was ready to retire. When I finished school and made the decision to permanently stick around, I wanted one place, one apartment, where I could live for ten years without moving. What a concept! As I'm writing this, I've lived in the same flat in North Beach for more than a decade.

Here's why I chose North Beach as a perfect place for retirement at the age of 21: great cafes, restaurants, bookstores. Great views, fresh air, not foggy. Culturally diverse. The only drawbacks were serious lack of parking, and, uh, that's all. After living in the Haight and a block from Telegraph Avenue in Berkeley, I was happy to not have my brain assaulted by screaming lunatics every time I stepped out of my doorway. Besides, being a writer in North Beach is a long-standing tradition.

Finding an apartment in North Beach happens like any other neighborhood: walk around and look for 'For Rent' signs. Up Telegraph Hill is pricier than down the hill toward Columbus and Bay Streets. North Beach also has cheap residential hotels, like the **St. Paul**, **Europa** (310 Columbus), **Golden Eagle** (402 Broadway), and **Entrella** (Columbus & Lombard) which are safer alternatives to similarly-priced Tenderloin accommodations.

Cheap eats are everywhere. **Golden Boy** (542 Green) Pizza's got the big honkin' slices, though **Viva** (1224 Grant) and **North Beach Pizza** (1499 & 1310 Grant) both have the tasty pies. The Vietnamese place just up Broadway from Columbus has $2 sandwiches served on a warm French baguette — but alas it's for meat-eaters only. Just up Broadway near Stockton is **Broadway Dim Sum & Cafe** which is open til 6:30 p.m. and dishes up huge plates of chow mein, ginger chicken over rice, and tofu beef over rice for $2. They also have enormous steamed chicken buns for 40 cents, and lots of righteous dim sum priced equally affordably. Try the shrimp har gow.

For a slight splurge, order the steamed clams in black bean sauce at **Yuet Lee** (1300 Stockton) on the corner of Stockton and Broadway. Or head over to **Little City** (Union & Powell), on the corner of Powell and Union, which has many incredible inventive dishes for under $10. Order the roasted garlic bulb for $1.25, it'll cure what ails you. Across the street is **Anthony's** (1701 Powell), where you can get a lobster dinner for around $10.

The **U.S. Restaurant** (431 Columbus) is absolutely godlike. The sandwiches on French bread are huge and accompanied by a pile of fries. Specials change daily, and on Friday nights, the red clam chowder and fried calamari rule. And the artichoke hearts sauteed in garlic are fantastic. For breakfast or brunch, the spinach omelette is superb, although it's more of a frittata than a typical omelette.

People always ask which Italian restaurant I'd recommend but since we eat pasta at home a lot, we rarely go out for Italian. For cheap pasta dishes, check out **Bocce** (478 Green) or **Pasta Pomodoro** (655 Union). For authentic light Italian, **L'Osteria** (519 Columbus) is great, though big eaters may still be hungry. The **Gold Spike** (527 Columbus) has a funky interior, and serves humongous, multicourse dinners for reasonable prices. The Friday night Crab Cioppino is highly recommended, and no one ever leaves hungry. If you don't mind cooking, stop by **Molinari's Delicatessen** (373 Columbus) and pick up some fresh pasta or ravioli. They make great deli sandwiches for a picnic in Washington Square Park, and have decent prices on chianti, olive oil, and fresh ground parmesan cheese.

Stockton Street in **Chinatown** has incredible prices on fruits and vegetables, as well as condiments like soy sauce, oyster sauce, etc. Also, save money on ramen noodles by buying the ramen-like egg noodle 8-pack for 59 cents at most groceries on Stockton Street. A few doors down from Columbus on Stockton, four bars of sandalwood and ginseng soap cost for $1. Across from the Walgreens on Stockton, there's a sort of Chinese Woolworths, which has tons of cheap stuff — I got an awesome umbrella there for $1.99.

As far as the cafes go, take your pick. They all have different personalities, which come from the owners and the people who hang out there. For really good coffee, I think the **Caffe Trieste** (601 Vallejo) rules. They roast the espresso beans right there (well, actually next door at the retail store), and the recognizable aroma often wafts through North Beach. The Trieste also has bizarre clientele, many of whom are marginally notorious. Keep an eye out for Gregory Corso. It's the only cafe that's been around since the '50s, and it shows.

Grant Avenue has some other cool stuff, like **Quantity Postcards** (1441 Grant). The walls are covered with thousands of purchasable out-to-lunch and traditional postcards, and some go for as little as ten cents. Down the street is **Figoni Hardware** (1351 Grant), an old-fashioned hardware store that totally rocks. They're got everything from furnace filters to pressed glass butter dishes, flower seeds, and duct tape. Nuts and bolts, too. **Yone** (478 Union) is a famous bead store on Union right above Grant for those into making their own accessories. There are a ton of other shops selling clothes, chotchkas, records, etc. but these are my favorites.

Also, an incredible North Beach only place is **Liguria Bakery** (1700 Stockton) at the corner of Stockton and Filbert. They only sell foccacia bread, but in four different flavors: plain, raisin, green onion, and pizza (which is plain with tomato sauce on top). It's delicious and legendary and certainly worthwhile sampling. The **Italian-French Baking Company** (1501 Grant) at the corner of Grant and Union has incredible biscotti, as well as amazing hefty rosemary baguettes for 95 cents.

Don't forget to walk up Telegraph Hill and check out the WPA murals at **Coit Tower**. They're absolutely gorgeous, and the view from the top ain't too shabby either. On the other side of Telegraph Hill, walk down the **Filbert Steps**, a beautiful stroll down a thoroughly country-like walkway. An amazingly surreal flock of **wild parrots**, green bodies with red near their beaks, live around Telegraph Hill and North Beach. In October, they are often seen in the pine trees at Washington Square Park, eating the nuts out of pinecones. They squawk loudly, and can often be heard flying overhead. And everyday between 8 and 9 a.m. in Washington Square Park, elderly Chinese people exercise and do **tai chi** en masse — truly an unusual sight to behold, if you're an early riser. Rumor has it that Marilyn Monroe and Joe DiMaggio got married in the big church facing the Park (DiMaggio grew up in North Beach), but they actually got married at City Hall.

Of historical interest, **1360 Montgomery**, a cool art deco building, was where Lauren Bacall lived in the Bogart classic, *Dark Passage*. **1010 Montgomery** Street is where Allen Ginsberg was living when he wrote *Howl*. The old-fashioned green **Sentinel Building** (916 Kearny at Columbus) is owned by Francis Ford Coppola and his film company Zoetrope. Coppola often eats lunch at the ever-excellent Chinese restaurant **House of Nanking** (919 Kearny) across the street. **City Lights** Bookstore (261 Columbus) is described eloquently by Jon Longhi in his chapter on bookstores, so I won't go into detail here, except to say, GO! (They stock every Manic D Press title there.)

Nightclubs like **Morty's** (1024 Kearny), and the **Purple Onion** (140 Columbus) harken back to the era of Lenny Bruce and cool jazz. In fact, the Purple Onion is where Phyllis Diller got her start, and Maya Angelou sang and danced there in the '50s (and you thought she was just a poet).

Bars like **Spec's** (12 Adler) and **Vesuvio** (255 Columbus) are terrific on the weeknights, but weekends stink as the bars quickly fill up with suburban yahoos. There's terrific original photo of Charlie Parker playing somewhere in the neighborhood hanging on the wall in Spec's. Get a pint of Anchor Steam at Vesuvio as the sun is setting and sit by the window in the upstairs balcony and watch the Broadway lights come on. On weekends, go to **Mr. Bing's** (Pacific & Broadway).

Grant Avenue has tons of bars with music, most notably **The Saloon** (1232 Grant), which is the oldest bar in San Francisco, built in 1861. Most of the bars on Grant feature blues or basic bar-band rock, but the

Gathering Cafe (1326 Grant) has jazz on the weekends, and of course, on Saturday mornings the Caffe Trieste owners sing opera and show tunes. Loudly.

On the other side of Columbus Avenue is Russian Hill, which has its own historical stuff. Definitely check out the roof of the San Francisco **Art Institute** (800 Chestnut), which has one of the best views in the City. There's a cheap cafe with good food and a million dollar view up there as well. Around the corner, at 949 Lombard, is the house where **MTV's Real World** San Francisco segment was filmed. Whatta buncha dweebs! Anyhow, also nearby is the ever-charming **Macondray Lane**, which is most likely the car-less street that Armistead Maupin modeled the fictitious Barbary Lane on in his classic *Tales of the City*. And **29 Russell** (which is an alley between Hyde and Larkin, and Green and Union) was Neal Cassady's residence, where Jack Kerouac put the finishing touches on his novel *On The Road*.

What else? There's always more. North Beach, Chinatown, and Russian Hill offer endless exploration. That's why it's a great place to retire. At the end of Stockton Street, visit the **sea lions** that loll around Pier 39. I'm tellin' ya, at night when fog horns are bellowing in from the Bay, sea lions are barking down at the pier, and cable car bells come tinkling over the breeze, it's like being in a movie. Except better. Because this is home.

OTHER COOL STUFF NEAR NORTH BEACH

The **Wave Organ** is a human-built, natural sound machine with incredible views of Golden Gate Bridge. Nearby, the **Presidio Pet Cemetery** is one of the more upscale places to end up as a dead dog. **Winona Ryder** and Soul Asylum's lead singer Dave Pirner recently bought a house in the 2600 block of Union Street. **Marina Green** is a good place to fly a kite. And nearby, the **Palace of Fine Arts** (Baker near Marina Blvd) is a romantic place to have a picnic, but bring a sweater in case the fog rolls in.

NORTH BEACH

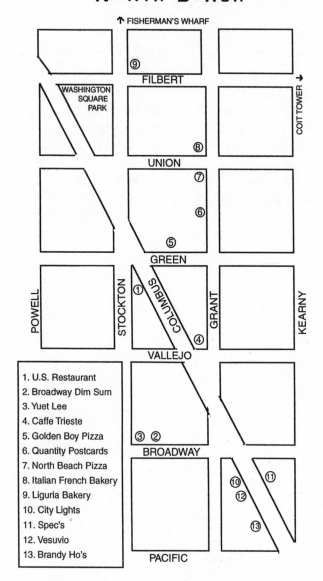

↑ FISHERMAN'S WHARF

→ COIT TOWER

WASHINGTON SQUARE PARK

FILBERT

UNION

GREEN

VALLEJO

BROADWAY

PACIFIC

POWELL

STOCKTON

COLUMBUS

GRANT

KEARNY

1. U.S. Restaurant
2. Broadway Dim Sum
3. Yuet Lee
4. Caffe Trieste
5. Golden Boy Pizza
6. Quantity Postcards
7. North Beach Pizza
8. Italian French Bakery
9. Liguria Bakery
10. City Lights
11. Spec's
12. Vesuvio
13. Brandy Ho's

THE INNER RICHMOND

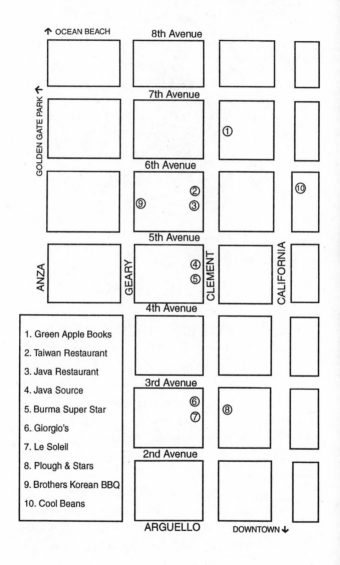

1. Green Apple Books
2. Taiwan Restaurant
3. Java Restaurant
4. Java Source
5. Burma Super Star
6. Giorgio's
7. Le Soleil
8. Plough & Stars
9. Brothers Korean BBQ
10. Cool Beans

THE RICHMOND, THE PARK, AND THE BEACH

BY MIRIAM WOLF

The Richmond District — or the "Upper West Side" as a friend refers to it because of its geographic location in the Northwest quadrant of San Francisco — is a neighborhood that doesn't get any respect. "Too suburban," the hipsters snort. "Always foggy."

Good. That just means its pleasures are more private.

The Richmond stretches 48 blocks, from Arguello to the ocean, from Lake Street to Fulton. It encompasses two of the more impressive parks in the U.S.: the Presidio (a former military base) and Golden Gate Park, plus a smaller patch of green, Lincoln Park. You can surf, swim, and sunbathe (in the buff at some locations) along the Richmond's well-kept urban beaches. It has touches of coffee house culture, as well as a varied immigrant population, with pockets of Russian, Asian, and Irish culture.

While the Richmond with its cookie-cutter stucco apartment buildings might seem drab compared to neighborhoods like North Beach, it does have one of the city's more fascinating attractions, one that's relaxing and sort of creepy at the same time: **The Neptune Society's Columbarium** (1 Loraine Ct., off Anza near Arguello). Housed in a beautiful four-story 1898 building, the Columbarium is a burial vault for cremated remains. Some famous San Francisco families have members in residence, including the Magnins (of department store fame) and the Folgers (think coffee). The niches are often decorated with icons that give a sense of the deceased's personality. One caveat here: go early, the Columbarium is open every day, but only from 10 a.m. to 1 p.m.

While you're in the inner Richmond, check out the absolute best of the city's bookstores (of course, I may be biased since I live four blocks away) **Green Apple Books** (506 Clement) is a fab place to browse for books both new and used. As soon as you walk in the door, that musty, mouthwatering "bookstore aroma" hits your senses and you start figuring out what percentage of all the money on your person you want to spend here.

After visiting the deceased and spending a few hours inside a bookstore, you might want to get a little fresh air. **Golden Gate Park**, a few long blocks from Clement, is a green, accommodating oasis. Sunday is a great day for a park visit — the main road, JFK Drive, is closed to traffic, making it a haven for bikers and in-line skaters of all ages and proficiency levels (pedestrians: take extra care in crossing).

The Park is also where you'll find a couple of the city's more respected (read: mainstream) museums. The **DeYoung Museum** specializes in American works. The **Asian Art Museum** boasts a fine collection of Japanese and Chinese works. Across the plaza, the **California Academy of Science** is where you go to play. It features a sizable aquarium, a planetarium, and cool exhibits like the one where you can experience an earthquake. Nearby, the **Japanese Tea Garden** is peaceful and meditative, while the **Strybing Arboretum** and the **Conservatory of Flowers** will tell you all you've ever wanted to know about the greenery. Of course, museums aren't cheap anymore, and even the Tea Garden charges an entry fee, so the thing to remember here can be summed up in three words: Free First Wednesday. Yes, the first Wednesday of every month, all the museums in San Francisco throw open their doors to the public, and forget to charge admission. Yes it's crowded, but for most of us, it's worth it.

In the mood for a not-too-taxing hike? You can follow the **Coastal Trail** from the end of the Marina, up though to **Fort Point** (with a cool view of the big orange bridge), and down the coast until you hit the parking lot for the Cliff House. Warning: Bring your own food! Do not eat at the Cliff House, which is overpriced and has only passable food (though at night, the bar is a nice spot for a (again pricey) cocktail.

While you're in the area, poke around the former **Sutro Baths**. Now just a hole in the ground, the Baths used to be the place for San Franciscans to socialize in swimming suits. You can also check out the **Musee Mechanique**, a museum dedicated to coin-operated amusement, from vintage peep shows (hot-cha!) to children's games. The **Camera Obscura** is there, too — a kind of giant camera that you can walk inside for a virtual look at the sunset.

Ocean Beach, which stretches from the Cliff House to Fort Funston is where you can catch some sun (if you're lucky), wade in the waves, see surfers (wearing wetsuits, of course — the water is damn cold year round), and see a wide variety of city dwellers getting sand in their shoes. Even on the coolest days, you can find people there walking dogs, playing catch, or just strolling along the surf.

Wanna get naked? Scenic North **Baker Beach** is a traditional (if not strictly legal) nude beach that attracts its fair share of crowds on the weekends. It's accessible by a trail that starts near Ft. Point and winds its way down the beach. Remember, it's not nice to stare.

Worked up an appetite yet? The Richmond has some of the best inexpensive restaurants in the city. You can get a good meal in most of the following restaurants for less than $10.

Khan Toke Thai House (5837 Geary), with its pretty good eats and on-the-floor-take-off-your-shoes seating, is a good bet if your want a "dining experience," not just a meal.

While we're on the subject of theme dining, **El Mansour** (3123 Clement) is a moderately priced (read:

not cheap) Moroccan restaurant, complete with belly dancers. Love the filo specialties.

Vietnamese? **Le Soleil** (133 Clement) has a delectable tofu with coconut milk dish that's rich and indulgent. **Taiwan** Restaurant (445 Clement) has Taiwanese specialties on the menu, along with more familiar Chinese dishes. It's busy on weekend mornings, when the locals crowd in for dim sum.

Do you like wheat gluten? The best fake meat in town can be found at the **Red Crane** Vegetarian and Seafood Restaurant (1115 Clement). It's a vegan's delight with dishes like sweet-and-sour-walnuts and snowpeas with vegetarian "ham."

The Richmond is an area full of bars, from the **Plough and Stars** (116 Clement) where Guinness is the drink of choice and traditional Irish music creates a good atmosphere for a game of darts, to **Pat O'Shea's Mad Hatter** (5848 Geary), an always-crowded sports bar. But you'll need a proper base for your beer. That's where **Giorgio's** (151 Clement) comes in, with it's heavy but yummy calzones, stabilizing garlic bread, and massive salads.

Get wired for a day of shopping with a shot of espresso from one of the many cafes in the Richmond. There's the tiny, funky **Cool Beans** (4342 California); the cavernous hangout **Java Source** (343 Clement) with its poetry readings every Tuesday night; **I Love Chocolate** (397 Arguello), which has the best brownies in town; or the **Blue Monkey** (1777 Steiner), built on the site of the infamous Winterland Auditorium) which blurs the line between inside and outside when it opens its windowed facade on sunny days.

BUCKETFUL O' BERKELEY

BY LISA TAPLIN

Berkeley is usually associated with the University of California and the '60s, which is a mistake because the city is so much more than just the school and its politics. While famous for its activism and socialist spirit, there is certainly more to do than go to a rally or sign petitions. The University itself offers great art exhibits, performances, and the best radio station you'll ever lay ears on. Campanile Tower is a constant landmark of academia and cultural resource, but Berkeley itself has enough character and oddity to keep you oblivious to the hordes of students and virtually nonexistent parking. It is a unique relationship that breeds an uncommon sense of community and eccentricity: the street people are more well-known than the University president, and the blooming wisteria often commands more attention that the picket signs. Whatever your interest, Berkeley has a wide range of resources, from traditional to way-out weird.

When I moved here nearly four years ago, I was instantly taken by the Berkeley's surreal contrasts: hulking houses perched on the hills; political slogans spraypainted on wooden gates; Telegraph Avenue's revolutionary spirit replaced by unabashed consumerism; sculptures made of trash placed in the shore flats of the Bay. The longer you're here, the more you uncover.

Berkeley is divided up into several residential and shopping areas: North, South and West Berkeley, the Berkeley Hills, downtown (where Shattuck and University Avenues meet), Telegraph Avenue (from Bancroft to Dwight Avenue), College Avenue, and Albany (which is its own small city, but is considered a Berkeley extension for all intensive purposes). Each area has its own neighborhood feel, cost of living, and hidden secrets. Generally, if you want to shop and 'check out the scene', go to Telegraph Avenue. If you want to experience Berkeley's Gourmet Ghetto, go to Shattuck Avenue in North Berkeley. These areas are the most touristy and are interesting in there own way, but the true fun of Berkeley is embedded in the rest of the city.

SHOPPING

If you decide to check out Berkeley's consumer culture but are looking for something more than standard fare trinkets, check out **Urban Ore** (7th & Gilmore). Its nearly an entire block of yard-sale oddities and a salvage-yard treasure chest. My favorite items there are the photographs from long-lost family albums, the rows of old claw-foot bathtubs, and shelves upon shelves of random electronic junk. Its a pack-rat's paradise!

The **Ashby Flea Market** (Ashby BART Parking Lot, Ashby & MLK) is a bargain-hunter's dream every Saturday and Sunday, complete with burning incense, reggae and hot dogs. You'll find every conceivable item here from bikes, Super-8 cameras and belt buckles to natural remedies, Oriental rugs, and old blues albums.

The Bay Area seems to have a culture all its own, and you can check out a lot of it at **La Pena Cultural Center** (3105 Shattuck). The storefront offers hard to find books by a diverse selection of authors, focusing on Latin and Central America. They have a great selection of CDs and tapes from traditional folk singers to spoken word artists. The Center also sponsors talks, political rallies and performances to keep you up to speed with the goings on in the local community and the rest of the world. On weekend nights, they offer salsa lessons and dancing to live local and national bands.

When you feel the need to become more political or are determined to stop the world from going to hell in a handbasket, cross the street to **The Long Haul Bookstore** (3124 Shattuck). Chat with local activists as you browse through their collection of political and social action titles. Get involved in current events and plan your own revolution. This is the place to dig in...

Speaking of digging, the **Bone Room** (1569

Solano Ave, Albany) dedicates itself to the joy of human and animal skeletons. Wonder over the insides of a cat or check out their insect collection. They will fulfill your need for increased calcium.

If you prefer living beings, the **Vivarium** (1827 5th St) has over 200 varieties of snakes, lizards, turtles and insects to entertain you. I dare you to go into this place and not come out with a baby Bearded Dragon lizard. It's a great place to buy your first lizard or to cure your fear of snakes. Mice, crickets, worms and other foodstuffs are for sale here as well.

If you're looking for clothing, whether it's a tie-dye, a Sari or a tiny tee, Telegraph Avenue is your best bet. My favorites are **Sharks** (2505 Telegraph) and **Wasteland** (2398 Telegraph). Both have a great selection of good quality inexpensive used and vintage clothing for any taste. The **Surplus Center** (1713 University), while far from Telegraph, offers basic Army/Navy standards (boots, coats and bags) at good prices.

For a unique book-buying experience try **Dark Carnival** (3086 Claremont) . Known for their large selection of oddities, this bookstore will satisfy your need for the off-beat literary experience. Science fiction, small press and wide releases can all be found here.

For a more graphic literary experience check out **Comic Relief** (2138 University). They offer every comic you could think of, including underground and local zines and mini-comics. The staff is friendly and knowledgeable and will help you find the release date for your favorite erratically published zine or refer you to particularly interesting artists and writers.

Cody's (2454 Telegraph) and **Moe's** (2476 Telegraph) are the two big bookstores on Telegraph Avenue that are able to maintain a small shop atmosphere. Both offer readings from every genre in the literary world along with their huge selection of books. Cody's has a large magazine room and carries several zines and small press publications. Moe's offers a great used book selection along with their shelves of new releases.

Small Press Distribution (1814 San Pablo) is more than a bookstore, because they distribute these books far and wide from their small storefront operation. It's one of the best ways to expand your literary horizons and see what's happening with alternative literary presses.

If you want large selection and bargain bins, **Half Price Books** (1849 Solano and 2525 Telegraph) is where paperbacks rule. With titles on nearly every subject, you're sure to find a suitable book at a decent price.

Mod Lang (2136 University) and **Amoeba Music** (2455 Telegraph) are the best places to buy new and used music. Mod Lang is the only place I would ever buy anything on an employee's recommendation. This tiny store carries an incredible collection of '60s psychedelic as well as techno, alternative, and rock. They specialize in CDs, but do carry records. You can pick up local zines and 7"s here along with imports and European music magazines. Amoeba, on the other hand is nearly a half a block of CDs, records and tapes. They have a huge selection of used music and are a great place to find obscure bands or lost favorites.

One of the benefits to living in Northern California is our proximity to the local farms and an appreciation for all things cultural, organic and natural. Go to any of Berkeley's **Farmers Market** (Saturdays and Sundays on Center Street, Tuesday afternoons from 2 p.m. til dusk on Derby & MLK) and you'll discover the variety of produce, spices and other homemade treats local farms have to offer. Or if your tastes are a little more exotic, try one of the many Indian or Thai markets running along University Avenue.

If nothing excites you more than a well-lit grocery with rows upon rows of shiny packages and gleaming produce check out **Whole Foods** (3000 Telegraph), Berkeley's employee-owned natural foods co-op. You could spend hours in here sifting through natural remedies or buying your gluten in bulk. They offer meats and cheeses from organic farms as well as foods to satisfy the strictest vegan. If you become weary while looking for rennetless cheese, visit the in-house masseuse for a quick rub-down.

Berkeley Bowl (2777 Shattuck) inhabits the old bowling alley. Where the lanes one stood are now rows upon rows of gorgeous fresh fruits, vegetables, meats, and fish. This place is *very* popular and can be crowded and hectic, but it lends something unique to the public market experience that you just don't get from a typical supermarket.

When money's an issue, the **Grocery Outlet** (2001 4th St.) is your ticket to slightly 'irregular' but low-priced foods. There's not much consistency in what you'll discover there from day to day, but if the price is right, you're sure to find some use for it...

DRINKING & EATING OUT

Berkeley is, for all intensive purposes, a suburb of San Francisco. You get to live in a funky old house with a backyard, and your cat can go outside, but it's more difficult to walk around the corner to see a band or frequent a local bar like you can in the City. Berkeley's social scene seems to revolve around parties and going out to brunch and dinner, but there are good bars and clubs here too, despite what many may think.

The easiest way to find out what's going on is to check out the bars on Telegraph. Many restaurants double as music clubs at night. The better ones are **Bison Brewing Co.** (2598 Telegraph) and **Larry Blake's** (2367 Telegraph). Both have bands on selected nights and serve locally produced microbrewed beer along with the commercial favorites. While it's not on Telegraph, **Jupiter** (2181 Shattuck) is a great place to go for a beer with lunch or after work. They often have bands and you can usually find a place to sit inside or on the outside courtyard.

The **Ivy Room** (858 San Pablo) is the quintessential hole-in-the-wall complete with a flickering neon cocktail glass sign and motorcycles parked out front. With a pool table and the best jukebox in the East Bay, this place is one of my favorites.

For a completely different experience try **The Pub** (1492 Solano). This cozy English bar is a converted house and offers a wide array of tobacco products along with wine and beer. If you're lucky you can score a seat on the couch next to the fireplace, but the other tables aren't too shabby. Overstuffed chairs flank heavy mahogany tables with antique reading lamps. It's a great place to play a game of cards or Scrabble while sipping a pint of Guinness.

You could visit Berkeley for a month and eat at a different restaurant every day. We're the home of **Chez Panisse** (1517 Shattuck Ave), originator of California Cuisine. If you just *have* to go, skip the pomp and circumstance and eat at the cafe upstairs. You'll be served the same food at a lower price, but without the 'atmosphere'.

Another cool little dinner place is **A La Carte** (1453 Dwight Way). The key word here is tiny as the supper club has about ten tables. Great local jazz bands serenade you through your meal.

When all you want is good pizza, you could get a tasty slice at **Blondie's** (2340 Telegraph), but when you want a god-like meal, head to **Zachary's** (1853 Solano) for the most scrumptious deep dish pizza this side of Chicago. Try their awesome stuffed spinach and mushroom pizza. It's like more like a pizza cake. Well worth the price.

If you are looking for great food, but can't afford the California Cuisine prices, you'll have no problem finding suitable restaurants. One of my favorites is **Long Life Vegi House** (2129 University). With lunch specials as low as $4 and huge portions, you can't go wrong at this vegetarian Chinese restaurant. They have a huge menu including seafood and gluten/tofu dishes, as well as spicy vegetable and noodle plates. On Sundays, they offer a fabulous and cheap dim sum menu.

If you're desperate for a salad, **Cafe Intermezzo** (2442 Telegraph) is a mecca, serving up cheap, humongous bowls of greens to the thronging masses.

Juan's (93 Carlton) is by far the most authentic Mexican restaurant in Berkeley. While many local restaurants are frequented mostly by college students, Juan's is packed with local Mexicans. You can get a huge burrito for under $5 and still have leftovers for later.

The best Thai around can be found at **Won Thai** (2449 Sacramento). This unassuming little restaurant will surprise you the minute you meet the very enthusiastic owner. Won Thai wins local "Best Of..." surveys every year for their divine soup.

University Avenue is virtual showcase of the Indian presence and influence in Berkeley. Tucked amongst sari showrooms are a multitude of Indian restaurants. The dining options are endless from modest buffets to deluxe dining experiences complete with sitar players. The **Indian Cafe** (1810 University), combining an authentic lunch buffet with a casual atmosphere, is one of my favorites. The restaurant is built into an upstairs loft over a small Indian market. Check out the music room or the imported spices and incense before your lunch.

One of the big social scenes in Berkeley revolves around brunch, and with so many little cafes in town there's a lot of choices. My favorites are **Homemade Cafe** (2454 Sacramento) for their yummy homefries and tasty pancakes. It's a bright bustling place with quick service and a take-out menu.

For a more rustic meal, try **Ann's Soup Kitchen** (2498 Telegraph). With breakfast made to order and apple butter toast it's a great place for a quick meal before setting off.

The local king of coffee and tea is **Peet's** (2916 Domingo, 1825 Solano, 2124 Vine). With three Berkeley locations, this East Bay original sells several dozen varieties of freshly roasted coffee beans (their Costa Rican blend offers a hearty caffeine bliss) and black and green teas.

The **Tea Spot,** also known as Ann Kong's World Famous Bleach Bottle Pig Farm (2072 San Pablo) is a quirky social place for food and cafe drinks. On many nights you can sip your Au Lait to the accompaniment of local musicians and singers. It's also a great brunch and dinner spot.

Other great cafes are **Cafe Strada** (2300 College), where you can chat with UC students or just sit on the verandah and be seen. The **Mediterraneum** (2475 Telegraph) is wedged between the shops on Telegraph and offers the perfect respite from the chaotic world outside. The **French Hotel** (1538 Shattuck) in the gourmet ghetto is the favorite hangout for many longtime Berkeleyites. You're sure to dig up interesting stories and information about the city over an herbal tea.

CULTURE, ART & ENTERTAINMENT

Berkeley seems to breed film buffs, from dark room hermits to Kung-Fu film fanatics. **Looking Glass** (2848 Telegraph) offers darkroom rentals as well as photography equipment and classes. They are also one of the few places that will develop and sell color Super-8 film stock; **Berkeley Black and White** (801 Camelia) will handle all of your black and white movie and photographic film needs.

For such a small city, Berkeley has an unfathomable number of movie theaters screening every imaginable genre and style. My favorite place to go on a Thursday night is the **UC Theater** (2036 University) for the Hong Kong festival. This ongoing series shows everything from Jackie Chan classics and Jet Li kung-fu extravaganzas to modern Chinese camp and romances. The double feature is $6 and fills up fast. A current schedule of films can be found in their lobby or at cafes and restaurants around town.

The **Northside Theater** (1828 Euclid) shows a quality selection of recent limited and wide releases. You feel like you're hanging out in someone's rec room watching movies on a large screen TV, but the small theaters and cozy ambiance lend themselves perfectly to the films they show here.

The **Pacific Film Archive** (2625 Durant) screens a variety of historic, classic and art films from around the world. They maintain an on-site library of movies, and are dedicated to the study and preservation of film. They offer talks and workshops on film theory and study. Printed schedules can be found in cafes around town or as inserts in the *East Bay Express*, or you can call them for updated info.

When you want to escape reality in your own home, the best place to rent movies is **Movie Image** (64 Shattuck Square). Their forté is kitsch, craft and odd cult classics, and they even update their movie selection every month and distribute their movie index for easy reference! One of the reasons I love this place is because their business combines two tried and true

Berkeley aesthetics: triumph of the little guy through hard work, and exaltation of the little guy through oddity.

When you're sick of watching movies and itch to make your own, the **Media Center** (2054 University) will rent you a video camera for a day or a week. They will teach you video technique and editing and, if you're good, enroll you in their annual amateur video film festival. Both **UC Berkeley Extension** (510-642-4111) and **Vista College** (510-841-8431) offer filmmaking classes, as well, during the academic year. Call them for application requirements and fees.

Berkeley is a great place to see bands. Most of the venues are small and the local music scene is great. Bands like Primus, Green Day, Rancid and Neurosis are all from the East Bay. Cover charges are usually under $10 to see three or four bands.

When you're in the mood for punk 924 **Gilman Street** is the only place to go. The club is run as an all-ages collective, so expect the under-18 set and no alcohol. It's a small place, with not much furniture: a couple of couches and a stage. Since the stardom of several local Gilman bands like Green Day, this place has become a mecca for punk music lovers.

Berkeley Square (1333 University) hosts bands from all musical influences. One night you might find a mainstream metal band, another night, a modern jazz quartet. If you're under 21 you'll have to buy drink tickets at the door, but the shows are generally inexpensive and the space is small, so it's still a great deal.

For a more traditional experience drop in on **The**

Starry Plough (3101 Shattuck). This Irish bar serves food during the day and has rock and folk bands at night. They sponsor a darts tournament and Irish dancing lessons every week.

Ashkenaz (1317 San Pablo) and **Freight and Salvage** (1111 Addison) are true products of Berkeley history. Both are funky little venues with a political past. If you're in the mood for something different check the schedules for these definitive Berkeley originals for world beat, jazz, and a little of everything else.

If you happen to be around UC at noon on a Friday, wander over to **Sproul Plaza** (junction of Telegraph & Bancroft Avenues) and see what bands are playing for free. The shows are usually in the summer and the bands are announced on fliers and on the local radio stations.

During your visit to the East Bay you'll have to tune in a few of our world-famous radio stations. UC Berkeley's **KALX** (90.7) will inspire and entertain you as enigmatic DJs broaden your musical horizons. In a single set you'll hear surf guitar classics, modern jazz and the newest punk. Program guides are available from downtown cafes and on the UC campus.

KPFA (94.1) is a Berkeley original specializing in an alternative media view. The DJs and program directors use the medium to its fullest with radio dramas like *Joe Frank: Work in Progress* and talk shows showcasing important local and world activists, current events and music greats. Its public radio in all its liberal glory.

Berkeley has recently experienced somewhat of a radio revolution, with pirate radio stations popping up all over the dial. **104.1** seems to have caught the community (and the FCC) by storm and continues to operate from an undisclosed location in South Berkeley. DJs play their own records and have the freedom to say and play anything they want. NPR has nothing on these guys.

Outdoor Fun

Some of the coolest and interesting places in Berkeley are free, and usually not in the local guidebooks. The first place to stop and check out an alternate vision of the city is the no-name **Laundromat** (2051 University). A huge mural of a post-nuclear Berkeley futurescape adorns the entire west wall, above the rows of washing machines. It's a great place to ponder your future during the spin cycle.

There is this a sculpture on the corner of Dwight Ave and 6th St that just boggles the mind. Its a great lime-green iron blob, that appears to be a fish, a globe, a twisted spine, a skeleton, free-form ovary...

Behind **Golden Gate Fields Racing Track** (a weird place in itself) at the foot of Gilman Street, is an old landfill right on the water. It's great for biking or checking out old rusted out junk and refuse from years past.

If you're looking for a more natural experience, **the secret garden** (3013 Wheeler) is a great chance to peek into someone's backyard and appreciate the gardens that grace many houses in Berkeley. Open on Sunday afternoons, the owners open up their private garden to visitors. They have combined luxurious landscaping with fantastic iron sculpture to create an incredible backyard arboretum.

If you're really into peeking into people's backyards take a hike up any of the pedestrian paths that wind through the **Berkeley Hills**. I suggest driving, biking or bussing up Euclid Avenue. After you pass the tight curves past Eunice Ave, look on your right for small road signs among the trees. Redwood, Brett Harte, Easter and Rock are a few you'll find. Most are paved walkways between huge wood and brick houses, draped in cherry trees, rhododendron and rose bushes. Most of the plants and gardens are maintained by residents, so no matter which season, you'll find the foliage in various stages of growth and bloom.

While lawn bowling does not appeal to everyone, you can watch heated matches and even take lessons for free at the **Lawn Bowling Park** (Acton & Bancroft). It's a great place to soak in the sun and get tips from the senior experts.

If you need a little inspiration, Berkeley has a variety of activities and places to lift your spirits or rekindle your creativity. If you have a car or bike, some of the best rides are through the Berkeley Hills to **Tilden Park** (where Euclid and Grizzly Peak meet). There are few roads through this 2065 acre natural park, but if you follow **Wildcat Canyon Road** through the park and over the other side you'll be treated to a fantastic view of the valley on the East side. If you'd rather go for a hike, the park offers miles of paths of varying levels of difficulty through windswept hills, fragrant eucalyptus groves or thick forests. **Inspiration Point** offers a fabulous sunset or an ominous view of the incoming fog. **Lake Anza** is a great place for a swim in the summer, although it can may be crowded on weekends. The park also has a botanical garden, a merry-go-round, a pony ranch, and a small farm. Stop by any of the park buildings for more information about trails and activities. To get to Tilden by bus, hop on AC Transit bus #67.

If you're not up for the trek to Tilden, climb up **Indian Rock** (on Indian Rock Road, between Oxford and Shattuck) and join the regulars for the sunset show. A three-bridge view of the entire Bay is worth the scramble up the residential crag.

If views are what you're after, take an elevator ride to the top of the **UC Berkeley Campanile** tower. Some say it's an eyesore, many see it as a symbol of the city, but for only 50 cents, you'll get a great view of the Bay and SF.

The **Berkeley Rose Garden** (1201 Euclid) is guaranteed to soften your cynical heart and inspire thoughts of love. The best time to go is in the late spring and summer when the roses are in full bloom.

The **Berkeley Marina** (at the foot of University Avenue) is an interesting mix of local fisherman, exclusive yacht clubs, and parks. The park on the north side offers a great view of incoming ships and fancy kite flying. You can try your hand at windsurfing or buy fresh fish at the local market, but there's nothing nicer than a sunset stroll along the pedestrian path to the accompaniment of the Bay's foghorns.

Berkeley's denizens are entertaining enough on their own. If you stroll down Telegraph Avenue, take a peek into the stores and restaurants. You'll find some of the most beautifully inspirational people. **Whole Foods Market** (3000 Telegraph) is famous for its huge selection of natural and organic foods, but is notorious for employing and serving some of the best looking Berkeley inhabitants.

IF YOU DECIDE TO STAY

If after some time in the Bay Area, you decide to settle down and live here, you'll find Berkeley an easy place to settle into. If you're pressed for money or time, the downtown **YMCA** (201 Allston Way) offers single-sex and coed rooms at a good price. While you're staying there you might want to have a quick workout. The new Y is huge and offers 3 swimming pools, 4 work out rooms (including a women's only room), 2 basketball courts, aerobics, and handball courts. They are very generous with their financial aid, and you can generally get a membership for $20 a month, depending on need.

If you decide to take up more permanent residence, pick up an *East Bay Express*. This substantial weekly has extensive housing listings ranging from shared living and co-ops, to cottages, houses and sublets. You might check out **Homefinders** (2158 University) if you can't find what you're looking for in the paper. They offer listings based on your particular housing need for a monthly fee.

Once you've settled into your rent-controlled Berkeley bungalow, you're going to need a job. If you want to hone your computer skills and dig into the community go to **BMUG** (2055 Center). They offer all the information, resources and classes you need to master the Macintosh computer. A six month membership for $28 gives you access to their graphical

BBS, where you'll find job and housing listings, computer and social conferences, and a huge software library, all with a decidedly Berkeley flair.

The **YWCA** (2600 Bancroft) is also great job and class resource with listings and guidance on how to find your dream career, be it as a CPA or a bellydancer.

The **Women's Employment Resources** (3362 Adeline) runs a free service for job seekers. They have binders of job listings for both men and women, as well as support services from resume writing to career counseling.

Women Empowering Women (510-525-7645) is a unique organization offering apprenticeships in areas traditionally closed to women. They offer programs in carpentry, plumbing, electricity and auto repair. The classes are cheap and fees are based on a sliding scale.

TRANSPORTATION

Getting around Berkeley can be a problem. Don't drive if you can help it. The city has a horrible parking deficiency, and hyperactive meter maids. Most parking is on very time-restricting meters that operate on nickels and quarters only. (Dimes were eliminated when people were tricking the meters with filed down pennies.) Most residential areas require a permit if you want to park for more than two hours and many streets have street sweeping days once or twice a month. If you think you've found the perfect parking space look around for signs, because the meter maids will get you if you are parked illegally. The best places to park around Telegraph Avenue are the public garage on Dwight and the lot on Channing. Downtown Berkeley has several lots, the least expensive being the garage on Allston ($6.50 for all day) and the garage on Kitterage ($2 after 6 p.m.).

Berkeley has a great, though pricey, public transportation system based on BART and AC Transit. With three Berkeley stations (Ashby, Downtown and North Berkeley) BART is the best way to get to Berkeley from San Francisco, or the Oakland airport. You can get a transfer from the station and hop on an AC Transit bus, or pay the standard busfare of $1.15. Transfers last for an hour. For BART and bus schedules, go to **Berkeley TRIP** (2033 Center), a nonprofit organization dedicated to saving the Bay Area from single person automobiles. You can set up carpools, get bike maps, and figure out the 'greenest' way to get where you want to go.

Many people who live or work in Berkeley travel by bicycle. While the city has a noticeable lack of bike lanes, most drivers are aware and conscientious of bicyclists. The city is situated on a gradual upward slope that ranges from slight to drastic as you head into the hills. One of the first places you should go is **Missing Link** (1988 Shattuck). This bike store is run as a collective where you can take a free class on bike repair, or borrow their tools to do your own fine-tuning. They recently opened a used bike store across the street from their retail store. You can trade in your old decrepit monster for credit for a new (or used) bike. If you can roll it in, they'll give you at least $25 credit. If you have questions about interesting rides or local laws the folks at Missing Link will give you all the info you need.

You might want to participate in the Berkeley incarnation of **Critical Mass**, a monthly bicycle rally to promote the use of bikes instead of cars. Its a fun, politically charged, though leisurely, ride through the most congested areas of Berkeley. The riders hand out flyers about the harm of cars and the benefits of bicycling. The rally runs the second to last Friday of every month, starting at Downtown Berkeley BART at 5 p.m. The ride lasts about an hour and people generally split off for rides up to Tilden or down to the Marina.

When the traffic really gets you down, and you need to get far far away, call up **Green Tortoise** (415-821-0803). With cheap fares and a unique bus fleet, they will take you where you want to go in style. For less than $100 you can catch the bus at the Berkeley Marina and travel round-trip to Oregon. For a little more, you can travel to Mexico, Costa Rica or the East Coast, among other fabulous destinations. Green Tortoise owns several hostels and parcels of land, where you can rest your weary bones and have a hot meal, stop for a dip in a hot spring, or go for a hike. If you just can't go home, they're always hiring drivers for their wacky fleet of green busses.

UC Berkeley offers a variety of getaway trips through **Cal Adventures** (2301 Bancroft), including weekend mountain climbing, hiking and camping, sailing, fishing and rafting. Most trips or lessons start in the summer, but call them for seasonal adventure specials.

If a good book is all you need to spark your creativity, the **Berkeley Public Library** (Shattuck and Kittridge) offers up their volumes for you perusal. They sport a great music listening and lending library as well. All you need to get a card is an ID and letter addressed to you in Berkeley.

UNEXPECTED OAKLAND

BY DASHKA SLATER

Oakland is a city of pockets, of unexpected things. It takes a while to get to know it and a lifetime to understand it, but those of us who live here love it the way poets love poetry. We know the rest of the world considers us irrelevant, but we think we've found the key to everything.

If San Francisco is an international city, Oakland is an American one, as quixotic and perplexing as America itself. Oakland is America as it used to be: a city of railroads and shipyards. Oakland is America as it will be: neither white, nor black, nor Asian nor Latino nor Native American, but all of these together. It has sun in summer, 22 miles of shoreline, a redwood forest and a saltwater lake but it doesn't wear its attributes on its sleeve. When you set out to visit Oakland, you have to be a sleuth, because this is a city of hidden things, of dusty shops and secret passageways. Here are some clues as to what to look for, but the best things are the ones you find on your own.

BOOKSTORES

The Bay Area is filled with wonderful, well-stocked independent bookstores and Oakland is no exception. But the city also has an unparalleled selection of antiquarian bookstores, places filled with dusty treasures and strange serendipitous wonders, first editions, collections of ancient books on flying saucers and military history, and they are all scattered in and around downtown. The city's largest cluster of antiquarian booksellers is facing temporary relocation as their building is reconstructed, so you should check their addresses before showing up. But if you're lucky, they are still in the wonderful **Pardee Building** (16th & San Pablo), a combination of artist studios and bookstores with a barber shop and the city's only shoeshine stand thrown into the mix. Here you can find **Bibliomania** (1539 San Pablo) which specializes in books on social movements with things like anti-lynching tracts from the pre-civil rights era South, the collected works of Mussolini, in Italian, and a startling selection of books and pamphlets about flying saucers and other occultist movements. In the same building, the **Key Bookshop** (531 16th) specializes in Black Studies and books about Africa, and also has a great collection of cheap paperbacks. The **Gull Book and Print Gallery** (1551 San Pablo) is a consortium of 24 rare book dealers, which includes lots of literary first editions and western Americana. Former Pardee building resident **Dan Webb Books** has moved its collection of military books and regional American cookbooks to 15 Grand Avenue, near the corner of Broadway.

Not far from the Pardee Building is **De Lauer Super Newsstand** (1310 Broadway) which has an enormous selection of magazines and newspapers from all over the world and has the added advantage of being open 24 hours a day. Over in Old Oakland is the **Friends of the Oakland Public Library** store (815 Washington), with its ever changing collection of plastic-covered discards. This is a great place to find old children's books and tawdry romance novels . Veering even farther from the world of literature is the **Western Christian Bookstore** (1618 Franklin), a place which carries underground comics far more depraved than *Horny Biker Sluts*, for only twelve cents each. I'm speaking of the pocket sized comic book tracts from Chick Publications that explain how Halloween is a cover for Satanists who want to murder little children, how the Catholic Church is conspiring to bring communism and Mary worship to the world, and other little known facts. Just don't giggle too loudly while you're in the store, or they'll boot you out.

ART

With its big empty warehouses and low rents, Oakland is a perfect haven for artists, and it is rumored to have more artists in residence than just about any city in the country, with the exception of New York. It is also the place to get a feel for what California art is about, as opposed to that washed-out, bloodless stuff they import from New York and put in the SFMOMA. The **Oakland Museum** (1000 Oak St at Tenth) is the official Museum of California, containing the best and most extensive collection of California art from the age of exploration to the present. There are also history and a natural science departments. Between the three divisions there is always at least one outstanding special exhibition, and the permanent collections are well worth gawking at in and of themselves. Make sure to go through the little screen door in the main art gallery to see the miniature SoCal valley scene, complete with trailer, dump site and freeway noise. A few blocks away, the Oakland Museum's **Sculpture Garden** (1111 Broadway) is in the lobby of the American President Lines Building and has small, innovative sculpture exhibits in a sunny atrium gallery.

Pro Arts Gallery in Old Oakland (461 Ninth St) is the foremost gallery in the East Bay, with a different exhibit every month and a great gallery shop at the front. They also sponsor the East Bay open studio exhibit every June. The **Ebony Museum of Art** (30 Jack London Village, Suites 208-209) showcases African and African American art and artifacts, from 1960s issues of *Ebony* magazine to intricately beaded figures from Zaire and Cameroon. Most amazing of all is Aissatoui A. Vernita's spooky and beautiful soul food sculptures — a bench made out of beef shoulder blade bones, a church made of fatback, mustard and collard greens, and beef and chicken bones. In the same building is Samuel's Gallery which carries prints, limited editions and originals by more than 250 black and African artists like William Toliver, Ernie Barnes and Synthia Saint James. One of the best, and most unusual, places to see art is **Creative Arts Gallery** (355 24th St) which shows the work of "outsider" artists — artists with emotional or mental disabilities. The work is amazing — emotional, exuberant, humorous and utterly unlike anything you'll see anywhere else. Across the street from Jack London Square is the **Museum of Children's Art** (560 Second St), better known as MOCHA. The artists on display range from very young to high school age, but the art is always surprising — and often less childish than much of the stuff you see in the adult galleries. Mocha is also a great place to bring kids for hands-on art projects.

Sites, Attractions & Walks

If you come to Oakland during one of its many annual festivals, go out of your way to attend. The best is of course **Festival at the Lake**, a huge, three day extravaganza of food and music and crafts and all-around good feeling that happens every June. Other annual events are the **Black Cowboys Parade** (October), the **Greek Festival** (May) and the **Asian Street Fair** (August).

Don't be too disappointed if you miss one of the big annual events though, there's still a lot to do. The Rockridge/College Avenue and Grand Avenue/Lake Shore neighborhoods are full of cafes, bookstores and boutiques to check out, and if you enjoy fantasizing about how you would live if you had piles of money, the Trestle Glen neighborhood (just off of Lake Shore

Avenue) has acres of windy streets and lavish mansions.

The most famous walk in Oakland is the 3 mile walk around **Lake Merritt**, and for good reason. The Lake is the best place to get a feel for Oakland as a truly multicultural city and if you are the kind of person who gets pleasure from just seeing all the different shades and shapes and styles human beings come in, this is the place to do it. The Lake used to be a tidal swamp before it was made into a saltwater lake and it can get a bit smelly in summertime. Still, the scenery's pretty, and you can rent sailboats, paddleboats, canoes and rowboats at the boathouse. If you have a kid with you, you can get into **Children's Fairyland**, a decidedly surreal collection of painted storybook sculptures that speak with strange disembodied voices. Not to be missed, but they won't let you in without a kid in tow.

Keep your eye out for the low-lying labyrinth on the edge of the Lake; it looks kind of like a strangely symmetrical collection of rodent burrows. This isn't the kind of labyrinth you get lost in, it's more of a spiritual journey, for those who don't have time for longer pilgrimages. Walking through the pattern is supposed to be a form of meditation, so tell your traveling companions to stop blathering and see if you get hit by any blinding insights while you're walking.

A similar maze can be found in **Sibley Volcanic Regional Preserve**, on Skyline Boulevard just south of the intersection with Grizzly Peak Boulevard, but you have to look for it. On a clear day you can see Mt. Diablo from here, and in spring there are wildflowers tucked among the ancient lava flows. Just south of the entrance to Sibley is **Huckleberry Botanic Regional**

Preserve, a 132 acre self-guided nature trail where you can see a variety of rare native plants, including what the park district describes romantically as "elfin forests" of manzanita. Nearby, is **Redwood Regional Park**, the most popular of Oakland's wild parks because of its 150 foot redwoods and woodsy paths and gorgeous Bay views. In the afternoon, everyone and their dog seems to be here — literally. For some reason it is the dog-walking capital of the East Bay.

If you want to stay closer to the center of town, there's nothing like a long walk through **Mountain View Cemetery** (5000 Piedmont), culminating in a picnic on the front stoop of one of its residents' granite mansions. The 220-acre cemetery is filled with winding paths, surprising little lakes, and wondrous monuments to the self-important dearly departed, which is why it has become North Oakland's favorite (and only) park, filled with joggers and bicyclists as well as mourners. The dead don't seem to mind, at least I've never heard them complain, and you can't beat the view from the Crocker monument — the glistening waters of the Bay, the open palm of the flatlands above it, and the gray tombstones dappling the foreground. It's the kind of view that makes you glad to be alive.

Landscape architect Frederick Law Olmstead, best known for designing New York's Central Park, designed Mountain View in the tradition of the "garden cemeteries" of the east, but used plants like Italian cypresses and Lebanese cedars that were suited to the aridity of the west. The cemetery quickly became the East Bay's poshest final resting place, attracting the mortal remains of such luminaries as architects Julia

Morgan and Bernard Maybeck, industrialist Henry J. Kaiser, Emeryville founder Joseph Emery, chocolatier Domingo Ghirardelli, Chabot observatory founder Anthony Chabot, and Key System founder and washing products czar Francis "Borax" Smith. Perhaps the most egomaniacal of the notables interred there is temperance leader Henry David Cogswell, who had a 70-foot high granite obelisk erected over his tomb. The granite had to be brought from the East coast and at 329 tons was the heaviest shipment ever made at one time across the continent. It took 38 freight cars to carry it. While no one else can match this monument for heft, up on "Millionaire's Row" is a series of posh crypts that look exactly like a bunch of old mansions.

On the other end of the spectrum, **Evergreen Cemetery** (6450 Camden), is the final resting place for the remains of more than 400 unidentified members of the People's Temple, killed in the 1978 Jonestown massacre in Guyana. A simple marker shows where they are buried.

Up in the East Oakland hills is another great destination, the **Mormon Temple** (4770 Lincoln Ave), more often referred to around here as Oz, because when you look up at the hills at night you can see it glowing green. The Temple's visitor's center has a talking Jesus as well as other informative displays, not unlike the ones in Tony Kuschner's *Perestroika*. Ask a question, and you can hear the answer right out of the mouth of Our Lord. While you're there, you can take advantage of the genealogical library and look up your lost ancestors.

Jack London Square is both cool and bogus at

the same time, but there are ways to maximize the former and minimize the latter. It's cool to be on the waterfront, and cool to see the boats and the container ships and the pleasure boats, but most of the stores and restaurants are about what you'd expect — bland and generic. The waterfront goes on for 22 miles though, and if you know how to kayak you can rent a single or a double here at **California Canoe and Kayak** ($15 for singles, $20 for doubles) and tour the estuary yourself. The estuary is a wild place that includes a bizarre settlement of maritime gypsies and various other wonders, both natural and manmade — rusting barges and dilapidated warehouses, the race course for the Cal crew team, and a succession of drawbridges among them.

If you have to stay on land, the best time to come to Jack London Square is during the Sunday morning farmers market, when the whole place has a festival atmosphere. You can get all you need at the **Farmer's Market** to picnic by the water, but if you want prepared food, skip TGIFriday's and the other swill, and head over to the **Cuckoo's Nest** (247 Fourth St) where you can get sandwiches, polenta, espresso and a good selection of wine and beer in a gorgeous warehouse cafe. One touristy option that really is kind of cool is **Heinhold's First and Last Chance Saloon** (56 Jack London Square), which was once Jack London's favorite bar. A tiny little shed with more than a hundred years build up of cigarette smoke and stale beer smell, the saloon is still lit by gas lanterns and has a slanted floor brought about by the 1906 earthquake. A block away, tucked among the wooden walkways of Jack London

Village, you can view first editions of some of his 52 books at the **Jack London Museum** (30 Jack London Square). There are even a few cheesecake shots of a bare-bummed Jack, taken for his medical records.

Oakland is one of the largest working ports on the West Coast, but although you can see the cranes that look like immense horses from just about anywhere in town, there are only two places where you can actually see the cranes in operation, loading and unloading cargo from the container ships. One is at the end of Clay Street in Jack London Square, on what's called the **Roosevelt Pier**. The other is in **Port View Park** at very end of 7th Street, on a tiny spit of land that juts out into the Bay near the Bay Bridge. The view from here is spectacular, but it tends to be cold so bring a sweater.

Old Oakland and Chinatown are two neighborhoods right next to each other, in the area between 7th and 10th Streets. Old Oakland is on the west side of Broadway, Chinatown is on the east side, but both are great neighborhoods for just walking and exploring, either on your own or with a group. If you want a guide, call 510-238-3234 or 510-763-9218 to find out about the free walking tours that lead visitors through seven routes from May to October. Don't blanch at the word "tour" — these ones are very low key, and it's a good way to find some of the hidden spots — the beef jerky factory in Chinatown, for instance.

Chinatown is as much Southeast Asian as Chinese now, and unlike San Francisco's Grant Avenue it still functions as a residential neighborhood more than a tourist attraction. Here you'll find everything from a

Hello Kitty store to shops selling gnarled roots and powdery herbs, and ones selling silk dresses, plastic toys and handmade paper. Not to be missed is **Tin's Market** at 7th and Harrison, where you can find everything from tissue paper to shrimp chips to ginseng chewing gum. The best restaurants are **Vi's** (Vietnamese at 724 Webster), **Phnom Penh House** (Cambodian at 251 8th) and **Nan Yang** (Burmese at 301 8th). For Dim Sum, try the **Lantern Restaurant** (814 Webster) on Sunday mornings from nine until three .

If you prefer American or European cuisine, cross over to the Victorian-era streets and buildings of Old Oakland. At **Ratto's** (841 Washington) Italian deli you can get a sandwich to go, or during lunchtime hours you can hang out in the airy, high ceilinged dining room and make your selection from the cafeteria menu of pasta and gourmet sandwiches. A few doors down is **Caffe 817** (817 Washington) where you can get sandwiches, pastries and coffee, and if you're lucky enough to get an outdoor table, enjoy the sun. More outdoor tables are across the street at the **Pacific Coast Brewery** (906 Washington), which not only has a sunny beer garden and some of the best microbrewed beers in the nation, but it even has palatable pub food. On weekdays, the cheapest breakfast in town is at **Schiller's** (801 Washington), where you can plant yourself at the long yellow counter and order up a breakfast special — hotcakes, eggs, a side of ham, and coffee, for $3.30. The sunny, homestyle diner had its sign stolen years ago and never bothered to replace it, so you won't find it unless you know where to look: on the ground floor of the Oakland Hotel at the corner of

8th and Washington. Enter on the 8th Street side, the Washington Street door is always locked. An equally cheap lunch can be had at **Mi Rancho** (464 7th St), a Mexican grocery store and tortilla factory with a burrito counter in the back of the store.

NIGHTLIFE PERFORMANCES

If the idea of slurping noodles while a burly tenor is doing a Pavarotti imitation next to your table appeals to you, go to **Ratto's** (821 Washington) on a Friday or Saturday night for their Pasta and Opera night. For $22.50 you get a four course dinner and the pleasure of hearing opera singers belt out arias and even a few show tunes. Some take requests. The evening starts at 6:30; reservations are highly recommended: 832-6503

Chabot Observatory (4917 Mountain Blvd, near highways 580 and 13) has four large telescopes and a planetarium. On Friday and Saturday nights you can go up there, look through the telescope at the stars and planets or attend one of their planetarium shows (the shows always start at 7:30 p.m.). To find out what's playing at the planetarium, call 510-530-5225.

Built in 1926 and lovingly restored and expanded in the early '80s, The **Grand Lake Theater** (3200 Grand Avenue) is one of the best places in the world to see a first run movie It has electric fireworks exploding on its roof, faux marble pillars in its lobbies and Wurlitzer organ performances in the main theater before the show.

The best place to see an old movie is undoubtedly the **Paramount Theater** (2025 Broadway), a theater that is even more lavish than the Grand Lake. Like the

Grand Lake, the Paramount is an elegant old movie palace, with an immense elegant lobby, a glittering ceiling and a thousand other details that make you want to put on a satin evening gown and wear your hair like Veronica Lake. On selected Friday nights, the Paramount shows old movies complete with a short and a news reel, and even offers door prizes. The theater also has live performances by the Oakland Ballet and the Oakland Symphony, as well as various country, soul and gospel acts. To find out what's playing, call 510-465-6400.

Another great performing arts venue is the **Alice Arts Center** (1428 Alice), home of Dimensions Dance Theater and CitiCenter Dance Theater, the Oakland Ballet and the Oakland Ensemble Theater. Performances here are intermittent, but you can almost always take a dance class in one of the gorgeous old-fashioned dance studios — jazz, Haitian, Afro-Cuban, modern, ballet, salsa, hip-hop, flamenco, or samba. Call 510-238-7219 to find out about performances and dance classes.

For a full rundown of Oakland's theater, dance and music performances call 510-835-ARTS.

BARS AND NIGHTCLUBS

Oakland isn't a big nightclub town, and there is no place that counts as really hip. What the city has in spades is oddball bars that are sort of elegant and sort of divey and all in all seem to be not quite of this decade. My favorite is the **Terrace Lounge** at the elegant Claremont Hotel (Ashby and Domingo Avenues) because it has orange-hued fifties decor, a beautiful view of the Bay, and decent bands. Thursday night is swing night, other nights usually feature jazz or blues.

Down a peg or two from the Terrace's fusty elegance is the **Serenader** (504 Lake Park Avenue, near the Grand Lake Theater). Having been a speakeasy, jazz club and private home, this oddball bar has seen just about everything you can imagine, which probably accounts for the attitude of geniality. Some nights there's a blues band, some nights not, but the mood is always kind of hep. Further down toward the dive end of the spectrum is **The Alley** (3325 Grand), a hole-in-the-wall bar that's decorated like a cartoon alley, the kind where humpbacked cats yowl on fence tops and pawnshop windows advertise "Money to Loan." The bar's focal point is a large piano topped with a ring of microphones where would-be crooners gather to warble *Walking After Midnight* and *New York, New York.* House pianist Rod Dibble's style of play can only be described as plinking and most of the singers are in that middle stage of inebriation where they can remember the words but can't carry a tune — but hey, if you think you can do better, pull up a mike and sing it yourself.

Oakland was once the headquarters of the West Coast Blues, but there are only a few remnants of the old blues scene left. The most famous of these is **Eli's Mile High Club** (3629 Martin Luther King Jr. Way), a crowded, lively little bar that always has live music. The **Fifth Amendment** (3255 Lakeshore Avenue) isn't as historic, but it's in a similar mode — a cramped and smoky little blues bar that always has room for one more on the dance floor. For jazz, the best quality is always at **Yoshi's** (6030 Claremont), probably the world's only Japanese restaurant and jazz club, but the cover prices are steep so be prepared. For other entertainment listings, check out the *East Bay Express*, the East Bay's free weekly.

The East Bay has more brew pubs than you can shake a stick at, ranging from the sedate (**Barclay's** at 5940 College) to the loud and collegy (**E-line Ale House** at 5612 College). All are fine in their own way, but for something distinctive that caters to the slacker set, your best bet may be to forgo the bar scene altogether and go to **Your Mama's** (5239 College), a stylin' cafe that has espresso, beer and wine and a DJ spinning reggae, jazz, soul and hip-hop until 1 a.m. on weekdays and til 11 p.m. on weekends.

Speaking of Mamas, **Mama's Royal Cafe** (4012 Broadway) is the best place to go when you wake up with a sore head and a sour stomach the next morning. This restaurant has the most awesome selection of omelettes, the coolest waitresses, and the best decor in town. We're talking a mounted collection of old aprons and radios, a giant picture of buxom gals straddling baseball bats, and an ever-changing display of Napkin Art. There is always a wait on weekends, so bring the newspaper.

RESOURCE
REFERENCE

RESOURCE REFERENCE

TRAVEL & TRANSPORTATION

Airlines: Alaska-800-426-0333
　　　　　Southwest- 800-435-9792
　　　　　Tower Air-800-34-TOWER
　　　　　United-800-241-6522

Amtrak-800-872-7245

BART-788-227

Bus:　Green Tortoise-285-2441
　　　Greyhound-800-231-2222

Courier Flights: Jupiter-872-0845
　　　　　　　　UTL Travel-583-5074

Driveaway Cars: AAA Transport-342-9611

MUNI-673-6864

Rainbow Grocery -15th & Mission Sts. 863-0620

SamTrans-800-660-4287

Supershuttle-558-8500

LODGING

AYH-downtown 788-5604; Ft. Mason 771-7277

Avenue Hotel-524 Columbus & Stockton; 362-9861

Clift-Geary & Taylor; 775-4700

Europa-310 Columbus Ave & Broadway; 391-5779

Golden City Inn-1554 Howard (11th & 12th Sts); 255-1110

Golden Eagle-402 Broadway; 781-6859

Green Tortoise Guest House-490 Broadway;834-1000

Moffatt House-431 Hugo; 661-6210

Obrero Hotel-1208 Stockton; 989-3960

Phoenix Hotel-601 Eddy; 776-1380

Roommate Referral-610A Cole & Haight-626-0606

Sam Wong-615 Broadway & Columbus; 781-6836

San Remo Hotel-2237 Mason; 776-8688

SF Rent Board-554-9550

SF Tenants Union-282-6622

The Housing Committe-749-3700

Triton Hotel-342 Grant; 394-0500

EMPLOYMENT

Alumnae Resources-120 Montgomery; 274-4747
Experience Unlimited-745 Franklin; 771-1776
Foundation Center-312 Sutter; 397-0902
Media Alliance-814 Misson; 546-6334

CLOTHING, FURNITURE & STUFF

Big 5 Sporting Goods-2159 Chestnut
Black Market Music-1016 Howard
Buffalo Exchange-1555 Haight; 431-7733
Burlington Coat Factory-899 Howard
Busvan-244 Clement
Butterfield West-164 Utah at 15th; 861-7500
Clothes Contact-473 Valencia & 16th St; 621-3212
Community Thrift-625 Valencia
Cottrell's-150 Valencia
Depot-1st & Mission
Economy Restaurant Fixtures-1200 7th St.
Esprit-499 Illinois
Gap Outlet-2040 Chestnut
Good Vibrations-1210 Valencia
Goodwill-2279 Mission
Jessica McClintock/Gunne Sax Outlet-634 2nd St.
Loehmann's-222 Sutter
Marshalls-901 Market
Next Express-1315 Howard
Noel's Second Hand Appliances-3178 17th St.
North Face Outlet-1325 Howard
Personal Computers For Less-1309 Fillmore
Photographer's Supply-576 Folsom
Purple Heart-Mission & 15th Sts.
Ross-799 Market
Salvation Army-1509 Valencia
Shoe Pavillion-899 Howard
Sirius Connections-284-4700
Stormy Leather-1158 Howard
Subway Guitars-1800 Cedar, Berkeley
Thrift Town-Mission & 17th Sts.
Used Computer Store-2440 Shattuck, Berkeley

EATING OUT

Amazing Grace-216 Church
Annie's Seafood Bar & Grille-20 Annie
Bagdad Cafe-2295 Market
Bottom of the Hill-2742 17th St
Broadway Dim Sum & Cafe-684 Broadway
Burma Superstar-309 Clement
Cadillac Bar-325 Minna
Denny's Japantown-1700 Post
Eddie Rickenbacker's-133 Second St
El Rio-3158 Mission
El Trebol-3324 24th St.
Escape from New York Pizza- 1737 Haight & Cole; 668-5577
El Buen Sabor-699 Valencia
The Ganges-775 Frederick
Giladon Sushi-538 Valencia
Goat Hill Pizza-300 Connecticut
Golden Boy Pizza-542 Green & Grant; 982-9738
International House of Pancakes-2299 Lombard
Java-417 Clement & 6th Ave; 752-1541
Kate's Kitchen-471 Haight
King of Falafel-1801 Divisadero & Bush; 931-545
Kublai Khan's-1160 Polk
Kyoung Bok Palace-6314 Geary
L'Osteria-519 Columbus
Lucky Creation-854 Washington
Lucky Penny-2670 Geary
MacArthur Park-607 Front
Massawa-1538 Haight
Mifune-Japan Center, 1737 Post
Mission Villa-2391 Mission & 20th; 826-0454
Mo's-1322 Grant Avenue
New Dawn - 3174 16th St & Valencia; 553-8888
Nippon Sushi-316 16th St.
North Beach Pizza-1499 & 1310 Grant:433-2444
Now and Zen-1826 Buchanan
Original Buffalo Wings-663 Union
Orphan Andy's-3991 Market
Pork Store Cafe-1451 Hight

Pancho Villa's-3071 16th & Valencia; 864-8840
Raffles-1390 Market
Real Good Karma-501 Delores
Red's Java House-Pier 30 & Embarcadero
Roosevelt's Tamale Parlor-2817 24th St.
St. Francis Fountain-2801 24th St
Shangri-La-2026 Irving
Silver Crest Donut Shop-340 Bayshore
Silver Restaurant-737 Washington
Sparky's-242 Church
Ti Couz-3108 16th St
Tom Peasant Pies-4108 24th St.
Tonga Room-950 Mason
Two Jacks Seafood-401 Haight & Webster; 431-62
Truly Mediterranean-3109 16th
Tu Lan-8 6th St.
Umeko-Japantown
Video Cafe-21st Ave & Geary
Vietnam-620 Broadway
Yuet Lee-1300 Stockton & Broadway; 982-6020
Zante Pizza and Indian Cuisine-3489 Mission
Zim's-1495 Market & Van Ness; 3490 California

EATING IN
Cala-Haight & Stanyon
Castro Cheesery-427 Castro
FoodsCo-14th Street & Folsom
Grocery Outlet-1717 Harrison
Marina Safeway-15 Marina Blvd
Rainbow Grocery and General Store-1899 Mission
Trader Joe's-9th & Brannan Streets

COFFEEHOUSES
Caffe Trieste-Grant & Vallejo
Horse Shoe-Haight & Fillmore
La Boheme- 3318 24th St.
Sacred Grounds-2095 Hayes & Cole; 387-3859

BARS

Club Charleston-10 6th St.
Dovre Club-3541 18th & Valencia
El Rio-3158 Mission & Army; 282-3325
Mission Rock Resort-817 China Basin; 621-5538
Motherlode-1002 Post
San Francisco Brewing Company-155 Columbus
Spec's-12 Adler
Twenty Tank Brewery-316 11th St.
Uptown-200 Capp & 17th
Vesuvio's- 255 Columbus
Wild Side West-424 Cortland Ave.

FREE & CHEAP ENTERTAINMENT

Anchor Steam Brewing Company-1705 Mariposa; 863-8350
Ancient Tridentine Catholic Church-130 11th Ave
Angel Island-546-2628
Basic Brown Bear Factory-444 DeHaro; 626-0781
Bottom of the Hill-1233 17th & Missouri
Church of John Coltrane-351 Divisadero
City College-239-3000
City Guides-557-4266
DeYoung Museum-Golden Gate Park
Exploratorium-Lyon & Marina; 561-0360
Glide Memorial Church-330 Ellis
Golden Gate Fortune Cookie Factory-56 Ross Alley; 781-3956
Golf-666-7070
Japantown Bowl-Post & Webster
Kabuki Movie Theaters-Post & Fillmore; 931-9800
Museum of Modern Art-Van Ness & MacAllister
Public Library-Larkin & MacAllister; 557-4400
Rock'n'Bowl-1855 Haight & Stanyan; 826-2695
SF Ballet-Opera Hose at 401 Van Ness
SF Shakepeare Festival-666-2221
Steinhart Aquarium-Golden Gate Park; 750-7145
Stern Grove Festival-252-6252
Swimming Pools-274-0200
Tennis-751-7300
Yerba Buena Center for the Arts-701 Mission at Third St.

ENTERTAINMENT

SPOKEN WORD

Cafe International-508 Haight & Fillmore; 552-7390
Chameleon-853 Valencia & 20th; 821-1891
Jammin Java-Waller & Cole Sts.
Paradise Lounge- 15th & Folsom Sts.; 861-6906

BLUES

Blue Lamp-561 Geary;885-1464
Jack's-1601 Fillmore; 567-3227

DANCE CLUBS

Sound Factory-525 Harrison; 543-1300
Ten15-1015 Folsom; 431-1200
Townsend-177 Townsend; 974-1156
Trocadero Transfer-520 4th St.; 995-4600

JAZZ

Elbo Room-647 Valencia
Up & Down Club-1151 Folsom

ROCK

Bottom of the Hill-1233 17th at Missouri; 626-4455
Chameleon-853 Valencia; 821-1891
Covered Wagon-917 Folsom; 974-1585
DNA-375 11th St; 626-1409
Fillmore-1805 Geary; 346-6000
Great American Music Hall-859 O'Farrell; 885-0750
Hotel Utah-Bryant & 4th; 421-8308
Kilowatt-3160 16th St; 861-2595
Paradise Lounge-1501 Folsom; 861-6906
Purple Onion-140 Columbus; 398-8415
Slim's-333 11th St; 621-3330

RAVES

Housewares-1322 Haight

MOVIES

ATA (Artists Television Access)-992 Valencia; 824-3890
Casting Couch-950 Battery; 986-7001
Castro-429 Castro; 621-6120
Cinematheque-558-8129
Geneva Drive-In-587-2884
Kabuki-Post & Filmore;931-9800
Red Vic-1659 Haight; 668-3994

Roxie-16th & Valencia Sts.; 863-1087
Total Mobile Home Micro Cinema-51 McCoppin; 431-4007

THEATER, DANCE & PERFORMANCE

Climate Theater-252 9th; 626-9196
Cowell Theater-Ft. Mason; 441-3400
Intersection for the Arts-446 Valencia; 626-2787
Josie's Juice Joint & Cabaret-3583 16th St.; 861-7933
LunaSea-2940 16th St; 863-2989
Magic Theater-Ft. Mason; 441-8822
The Marsh-1062 Valencia; 826-5750
STBS-Stockton St., Union Square
Theater Artaud-450 Florida; 621-7797

POETIC EXPERIENCES

Aquatic Park - Beach & Hyde Sts. by the water
Golden Gate Park:
    Strybing Arboretum - near Lincoln & 9th Ave.
    Conservatory - near Arguello & Fulton Sts.
    Buffalo - near Fulton & 36th Ave.
Jack Early Park-Grant between Chestnut & Francisco
Ocean Beach - at the end of Golden Gate Park
Pier 47-behind Scoma's, Jefferson & Jones Sts.
Sutro Baths - near Cliff House & end of Geary Blvd.

HELPFUL & EMERGENCY INFO

City Animal Shelter-1200 15th St at Harrison
Consumer Action-777-9635
Consumer Credit Counseling-788-0288
Main Post Office-on Evans near 3rd St]
SPCA- 2500 16th St
Zip Code Info-284-0755
City Tow-1475 Mission
SF Dept of Parking and Traffic-553-1235
    Available 24 Hours:
Domestic Violence Hotline-800-540-5433
Gas Stations: 5th St & Harrison; 1st St & Harrison; Fell & Masonic;
19th Ave & Judah; Geary & 9th Ave; 19th Ave & Irving.
Pets Unlimited Vet Hospital-2343 Fillmore; 563-6700
Pharmacy: Walgreen's-498 Castro; 861-6276. 3201 Divisadero;

931-6415
Rape Treatment Center-821-3222
SF Women Against Rape-647-7273
Suicide Prevention-781-0500

HEALTH & WELL-BEING
AIDS Health Project's appointment line-554-9888
AIDS Info Hotline-863-2437
AIDS Services(San Francisco AIDS Foundation)-864-5855
AA-621-1326
General Hospital-1001 Potrero; 206-8000
Haight-Ashbury Free Medical Clinic-1698 Haight; 487-5634
Northern California Community Services Council-772-4357
SF Dept of Social Services-557-5000
SF Mental Health Association-921-4044
SF Neighborhood Legal Assistance Foundation-627-0220
University of the Pacific Dental School-2155 Webster; 929-6501
Volunteer Legal Services Program
Women's Needs Center-1825 Haight St; 487-5607

BOOK & COMICS STORES
Anubis Warpus-1525 Haight St
Austen Books-1687 Haight St
Booksmith-1644 Haight St
Bound Together-1369 Haight St
City Lights Bookstore-261 Columbus Ave.
Comic Relief-1597 Haight St
Comix Experience-305 Divisadero
Farley's-131518th St
Great Expectations-1512 Haight St
Green Apple Books-506 Clement St
Modern Times-888 Valencia
Naked Eye-533 Haight St
Pipe Dreams-1376 Haight St

TATTOOS & PIERCING
Body Manipulations-3234 16th St.
Gauntlet-2377 Market
Tattoo City-722 Columbus

KINKY SAN FRANCISCO

Cake Gallery-290 9th St; 861-CAKE
Campus Thater-220 Jones
Castlebar-552-2100
Don's of Sixth Street-111 6th St
1808 Club-1808 Market
Eros-2051 Market
Foxy Lady Boutique-2644 Mission
Good Vibrations-1210 Valencia
Lusty Lady-1033 Kearny
McB's Shoes-715 Market
Mr. S Leather-310 7th St.
New Century Theater-816 Larkin
Nob Hill Cinema-729 Bush
O'Farrell Theater-895 O'Farrell
Piedmont-1452 Haight
QSM-550-7776
Stormy Leather-1158 Howard
Tea Room Theater-145 Eddy
The Magazine-731 Larkin
Trocadero Transfer: Bondage-A-Go-Go/Ritual-520 4th St

QUEER SAN FRANCISCO
CLOTHING

A Taste of Leather-317 10th St
Aardvarks-1501 Haight St
Buffalo Exchange-1555 Haight St
Clothes Contact-473 Valencia St
Community Thrift-625 Valencia St
Crossroads-223 Market St
Held Over-1543 Haight St
Mr. S Leather-310 7th St
NaNa-2276 Market St
Salvation Army-1509 Valencia St & 1185 Sutter
Stormy Leather-1158 Howard
Thift Town-2101 Mission
Villains-1672 Haight
Wasteland-1660 Haight St
Worn Out West-582 Castro

BARS

Esta Noche-3079 16th St
The Cafe-Market & 17th
The Detour-2348 Market
The Eagle-Harrison & 12th
The Lone Star-1354 Harrison
The Mint-1942 Market
The Motherlode-1002 Post St
The N Touch-1548 Polk St
The Pendulum-4146 18th St
The Stud-399 9th St.

EATING OUT

Amazing Grace-216 Church St
Bagdad Cafe-2295 Market St
Hamburger Mary's-1582 Folsom
Hot & Hunky-4039 18th St
La Mediterranee-288 Noe & 2210 Fillmore
Orphan Andy's-3991 17th St
Sparky's-242 Church St

EATING IN

The Castro Cheesery-427 Castro
Harvest Ranch Market-2285 Market

DANCE CLUBS

Cat's Grill-1190 Folsom
Club Universe-177 Townsend
CW Saloon-911 Folsom
Lift-55 Natoma
Megatripolis-4th & Harrison
1015 Folsom
The Box-3rd & Harrison
The End Up-6th & Harrison
The Stud-399 9th St

SEX

Jaguar Books-4057 18th St
Le Salon-1124 Polk
The Magazine-920 Larkin
Campus Theater-220 Jones
Nob Hill Cinema-729 Bush
Tea Room Theater-145 Eddy

Good Vibrations-1210 Valencia
1808 Club-1808 Market
Eros-2051 Market
Collingwood Park-19th St & Collingwood
Delores Park-btwn 18th & 20th Streets, Dolores & Church Streets
Buena Vista Park-Haight & Baker
Corona Heights-Roosevelt & 16th Street
Dore Alley-btwn Howard & Folsom, 8th & 9th
Ringold Alley-btwn Folsom & Harrison, 8th & 9th

THEATERS & PERFORMANCE SPACES

Castro Theater-429 Castro
Roxie Cinema-3117 16th St
Rosie's Cabaret & Juice Joint-3583 16th St
Theatre Rhinoceros-2926 16th St
Victoria Theater-2961 16th St
Komotion-2779 16th St
Epicenter-475 Valencia
21 Bernice
Red Dora's Bearded Lady-4851 4th St
Cafe du Nord-2170 Market
848 Divisadero
ATA(Artist's Television Access)-992 Valencia
Theater Artaud-450 Florida
Intersection for the Arts-446 Valencia

ART GALLERIES

Southern Exposure-401 Alabama
Morphos-544 Hayes
Architrave-541 Hayes
New Langton Arts-1246 Folsom
Keane Eyes Gallery-651 Market

BOOKS & MOVIE RENTALS

A Different Light-489 Castro
Old Wives' Tales-1009 Valencia
Bound Together-1369 Haight
McDonald's-48 Turk
Leather Tongue Video-714 Valencia
The Gauntlet-2377 Market
Body Manipulations-3234 16th St

TENDERLOIN BAR CRAWL

Club Charleston-10 6th St
Peter Pan-45 Turk St
21 Club-98 Turk St
Club 65-65 Talyor St
Aunt Charlie's-133 Turk St
Coral Sea-220 Turk St
Kokpit-301 Turk St
Harrington's Pub-460 Larkin St
Brown Jug Saloon-496 Eddy
Jonell's-401 Ellis St
Cinnabar-397 Ellis St

THE MISSION

CLOTHING

Captain Jack's-866 Valencia
Community Thift-625 Valencia
Superthrift-560 Valencia
Thrift Town-2101 Mission

CAFES & BARS

Muddy's-1304 Valencia
Muddy Waters-521 Valencia
The Chameleon-853 Valencia
The Club-920 Valencia
Latin American Club-3286 22nd
Uptown-200 Capp

FOOD

Casa Sanchez-2778 24th St
Latin Freeze-3338 24th St
New Dawn-3174 16th St.
Mission Grounds-3170 16th St.
Pizza Pop-3274 21st St.
Truly Mediterranean-3109 16th St.
Taqueria Cancun-2288 Mission
The 16th and Mission Cafeteria-2022 Mission
Magic Donuts-2400 Mission

ENTERTAINMENT

Good Vibrations-1210 Valencia
Kilowatt-3160 16 St.

Roxie Cinema-3117 16th St
Leather Tongue Video-714 Valencia
Epicenter-475 Valencia
16th Note-3162 16th St
Balmy Alley-off 24th St between Treat & Harrison
Clarion Alley-between Mission & Valencia, 17th & 18th Sts
Emma Goldman's Home-569 Dolores
Botanica Yoruba-998 Valencia

THE HAIGHT
EATING OUT
All You Knead-1466 Haight
Dish-Haight & Masonic
Pork Store Cafe-1451 Haight
Studio Cafe-248 Fillmore
Kate's Kitchen-471 Haight
Spaghetti Western-576 Haight
Cha Cha Cha-1805 Haight
El Balazo-1654 Haight
Massawa-1538 Haight
Cybelle's-1535 Haight
People's Cafe-1419 Haight
Kan Zaman-1973 Haight
EATING IN
Haight Street Natural Foods-1621 Haight
Real Foods-1023 Stanyan
CLOTHING
Buffalo Exchange-1555 Haight
Wasteland-1660 Haight
Villains-1672 Haight
Backseat Betty-1590 Haight
STUFF
Pipe Dreams-1376 Haight
Housewares-1322 Haight
Behind The Post Office-1504 Haight
Rough Trade-1529 Haight
Recycled Records-1377 Haight
Reckless Records-1401 Haight
Gabardine's-342 Divisadero

NIGHTLIFE

Gold Cane-1569 Haight
The Deluxe-1511 Haight
Trax-1437 Haight
Nightbreak-1821 Haight
Murio's Trophy Room-1811 Haight
Persian Aub Zam Zam-1633 Haight
Nickie's Barbecue-460 Haight
Toronado-547 Haight
Mad Dog In The Fog-530 Haight
Armadillo-200 Fillmore
The Top-424 Haight

CAFES

Horse Shoe-566 Haight
Cafe International-508 Haight
Bean Bag-601 Divisadero
Coffee Zone-1409 Haight

NORTH BEACH

LODGING

Europa-310 Columbus
St. Paul-Kearny & Columbus
Golden Eagle-402 Broadway
Entrella-Columbus & Lombard

FOOD

Golden Boy Pizza-542 Green
Viva Pizza-1224 Grant
North Beach Pizza-1499 & 1310 Grant
Broadway Dim Sum & Cafe-Broadway near Stockton
Caffe Trieste-601 Vallejo
Liguria Bakery-1700 Stockton
Italian-French Baking Company-1501 Grant
Yuet Lee-1300 Stockton
Little City-Union & Powell
Anthony's-1701 Powell
U.S. Restaurant-431 Columbus
Bocce-478 Green
Pasta Pomodoro-655 Union
L'Osteria-519 Columbus

Gold Spike-527 Columbus
Molinari's Delicatessen-373 Columbus
House of Nanking-919 Kearny

STUFF
Quantity Postcards-1441 Grant
Figoni Hardware-1351 Grant
Yone-478 Union

NIGHTLIFE
Morty's-1024 Kearney
Purple Onion-140 Columbus
Spec's-12 Adler
Vesuvio-255 Columus
Mr. Bing's-Pacific & Broadway
The Saloon-1232 Grant
The Gathering Cafe-1326 Grant

THE RICHMOND, THE PARK & THE BEACH
FOOD
Khan Toke Thai House-5837 Geary
El Mansour-3123 Clement
Le Soleil-133 Clement
Taiwan-445 Clement
Red Crane-1115 Clement

BARS
Plough & Stars-116 Clement
Pat O'Shea's Mad Hatter-5848 Geary
Giorgio's-151 Clement

CAFES
Cool Beans-4342 California
Java Source-343 Clement
I Love Chocolate-397 Arguello
Blue Monkey-1777 Steiner

BERKELEY
STUFF
Urban Ore-7th & Gilman
Ashby Fleamarket-Ashby BART Parking Lot, Ashby & MLK
La Pena Cultural Center-3105 Shattuck
Long Haul Bookstore-3124 Shattuck

Bone Room-1569 Solano Ave, Albany
The Vivarium-1827 5th St
Sharks-2505 Telegraph
Wasteland-2398 Telegraph
Surplus Center- 1713University
Dark Carnival-3086 Claremont Ave
Comic Relief-2138 University
Cody's-2454 Telegraph
Moe's-2476 Telegraph
Small Press Distribution-1814 San Pablo
Half Price Books-1849 Solano & 2525 Telegraph
Mod Lang-2136 University
Amoeba Music-2455 Telegraph

DRINKING & EATING OUT

Bison Brewing Co.-2598 Telegraph
Larry Blake's-2367 Telegraph
Jupiter-2181 Shattuck
Ivy Room-858 San Pablo
The Pub-1492 Solano
Chez Panisse-1517 Shattuck
A La Carte-1453 Dwight Way
Blondie's-2340 Telegraph
Zachary's-1853 Solano
Long Life Veggie House-2129 University Ave
Juan's-93 Carleton
Won Thai-2449 Sacramento
Indian Cafe-1810 University Ave
Homemade Cafe-2454 Sacramento
Ann's Soup Kitchen-2498 Telegraph
Peet's-2916 Domingo,1825 Solano,2124 Vine
The Tea Spot-2072 San Pablo
Cafe Strada-2300 College
The Mediterraneum-2475 Telegraph
The French Hotel-1538 Shattuck
Cafe Intermezzo-2442 Telegraph

EATING IN

Whole Foods-3000 Telegraph
Berkeley Bowl-2777 Shattuck
Grocery Outlet-2001 4th St

CULTURE, ART & ENTERTAINMENT
Looking Glass-2848 Telegraph
Berkeley Black and White-801 Camelia
UC Theater-2036 University
Northside Thater-1828 Euclid
Pacific Film Archive-2625 Durant
Movie Image-64 Shattuck Square
Media Center-2054 University
UC Berkeley Extension-510-642-4111
Vista College-510-841-8431
924 Gilman Street
Berkeley Square-1333 University
Starry Plough-3101 Shattuck
Ashkenaz-1317 San Pablo
Freight and Salvage-1111 Addison
Sproul Plaza-Telegraph at Bancroft
KALX-90.7
KPFA-94.1
Radio Free Berkeley/Oakland-104.1

LODGING & EMPLOYMENT
YMCA-201 Allston Way
Homefinders-2158 University
BMUG-2055 Center St
YWCA-2600 Bancroft
Women's Employment Resources-3362 Adeline
Women Empowering Women-510-525-7645

TRANSPORTATION
Berkeley TRIP-2033 Center
Missing Link-1988 Shattuck
Green Tortoise-415-821-0803
Cal Adventures-2301 Bancroft

OAKLAND
BOOKSTORES
Pardee Building-16th & San Pablo
Bibliomania-1539 San Pablo
Key Bookshop-531 16th
Gull Book and Print Gallery-1551 San Pablo
Dan Webb Books-15 Grand Ave

De Lauer Super Newsstand-1310 Broadway
Friends of the Oakland Public Library Store-815 Washington
Western Christian Bookstore-1618 Franklin

MUSEUMS & GALLERIES

Oakland Museum-1000 Oak St at 10th
Sculpture Garden-1111 Broadway
Pro Arts Gallery-461 9th St
Ebony Museum of Art-30 Jack London Village
Creative Arts Gallery-355 24th St
Museum of Children's Art-560 2nd St
Jack London Museum-30 Jack London Square
Chabot Observatory-4917 Mountain Blvd
Grand Lake Theater-3200 Grand Ave.
Paramount Theater-2025 Broadway
Alice Arts Center-1428 Alice St

NIGHTLIFE

Terrace Lounge-Claremont Hotel, Ashby at Domingo
Serenader-504 Lake Park
The Alley-3325 Grand
Eli's Mile High Club-3629 Martin Luther King Jr. Way
Fifth Amendment-3255 Lakeshore Ave.
Yoshi's-6030 Claremont

RESTAURANTS, CAFES & BARS

Cuckoo's Nest-247 4th St
Heinhold's First and Last Chance Saloon-56 Jack London Square
Vi's-724 Webster
Phnom Penh House-251 8th
Nan Yang-301 8th
Lantern Restarant-814 Webster
Ratto's-841 Washington
Caffe 817-510-271-7965
Pacific Coast Brewery-906 Washington St
Schiller's-510-893-5408
Oakland Hotel-8th & Washington
Mi Rancho-464 7th St
Barclay's-5940 College Ave
E-line Ale House-5612 College Ave
Your Mama's-5239 College Ave
Mama's Royal Cafe-4012 Broadway

NOTES

Manic D Press
Books

Revival: spoken word from Lollapalooza 94.
*Edited by Juliette Torrez, Liz Belile,
Mud Baron & Jennifer Joseph.* $12.95

The Ghastly Ones & Other Fiendish Frolics.
Richard Sala. $9.95

The Underground Guide to San Francisco.
Jennifer Joseph, editor. $10.95

King of the Roadkills.
Bucky Sinister. $9.95

Alibi School.
Jeffrey McDaniel. $8.95

Signs of Life: channel-surfing through '90s
culture. *Edited by Jennifer Joseph &
Lisa Taplin.* $12.95

Beyond Definition: new writing from gay &
lesbian san francisco. *Edited by Marci
Blackman & Trebor Healey.* $10.95

Love Like Rage.
Wendy-o Matik $7.00

The Language of Birds.
Kimi Sugioka $7.00

The Rise and Fall of Third Leg.
Jon Longhi $9.95

Specimen Tank.
Buzz Callaway $10.95

The Verdict Is In.
> *Edited by Kathi Georges & Jennifer Joseph* $9.95

Elegy for the Old Stud.
> *David West* $7.00

The Back of a Spoon.
> *Jack Hirschman* $7.00

Mobius Stripper.
> *Bana Witt* $8.95

Baroque Outhouse/The Decapitated Head of a Dog. *Randolph Nae* $7.00

Graveyard Golf and other stories.
> *Vampyre Mike Kassel* $7.95

Bricks and Anchors.
> *Jon Longhi* $8.00

The Devil Won't Let Me In.
> *Alice Olds-Ellingson* $7.95

Greatest Hits.
> *Edited by Jennifer Joseph* $7.00

Lizards Again.
> *David Jewell* $7.00

The Future Isn't What It Used To Be.
> *Jennifer Joseph* $7.00

Acts of Submission.
> *Joie Cook* $4.00

Zucchini and other stories.
> *Jon Longhi* $3.00

Please add $2.00 to all orders
for postage and handling.

Manic D Press
Box 410804
San Francisco CA 94141 USA

manicd@sirius.com
http://www.well.com/user/manicd/

distributed to the trade
in the US & Canada by
Publishers Group West

in the UK & Europe by
Turnaround Distribution

in Australia by
Marginal Ex-poseur